PIANO • VOCAL • GUITAR

The Love Songs of
ELTON JOHN

Cover photo: Photofest

ISBN 978-1-61780-395-6

HAL•LEONARD
CORPORATION

7777 W. BLUEMOUND RD. P.O. BOX 13819 MILWAUKEE, WI 53213

Visit Hal Leonard Online at
www.halleonard.com

contents

Love

Songs

BELIEVE

Words and Music by ELTON JOHN
and BERNIE TAUPIN

Slow Rock Ballad

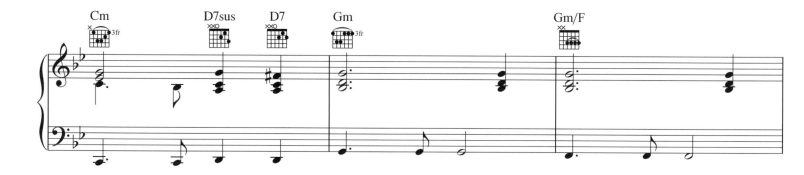

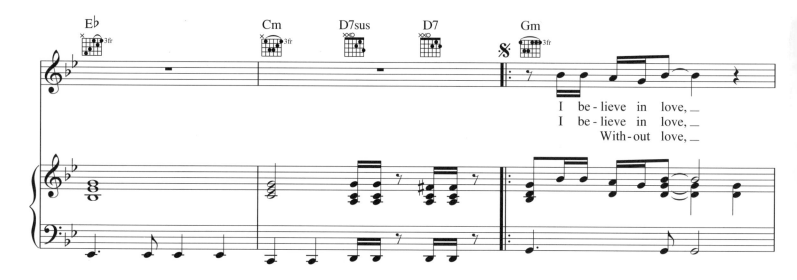

I be - lieve in love, __
I be - lieve in love, __
With - out love, __

it's all we've got. __ Love has no bound - 'ries, costs noth - ing to touch. __
it's all we've got. __ Love has no bound - 'ries, no bor - ders to cross. __
I would - n't be - lieve in an - y - thing __ that lives and breathes. _

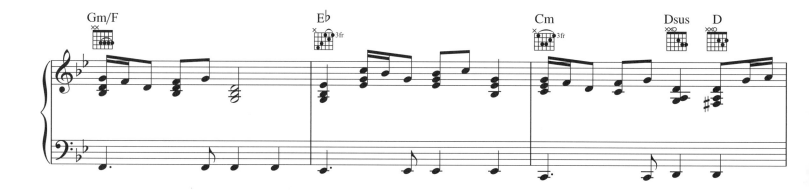

D.S. al Coda

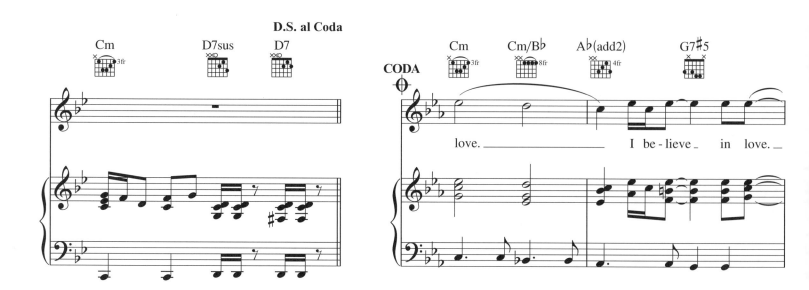

love. _____ I be-lieve _ in love. _

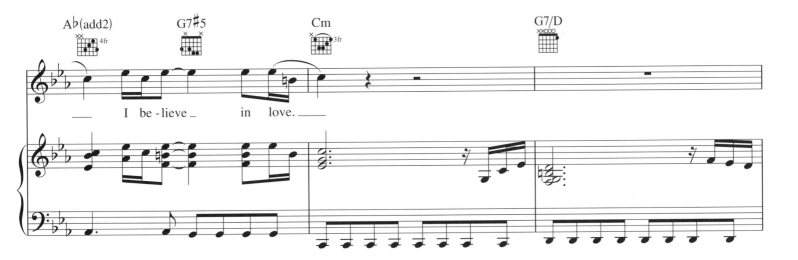

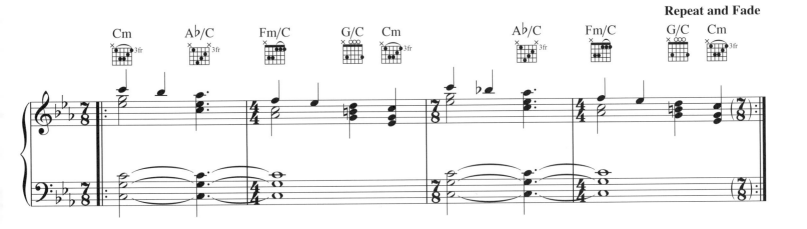

BLUE EYES

Words and Music by ELTON JOHN
and GARY OSBORNE

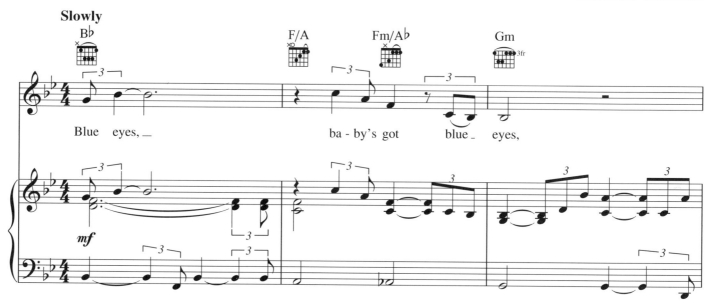

Blue eyes, ___ ba-by's got blue ___ eyes,

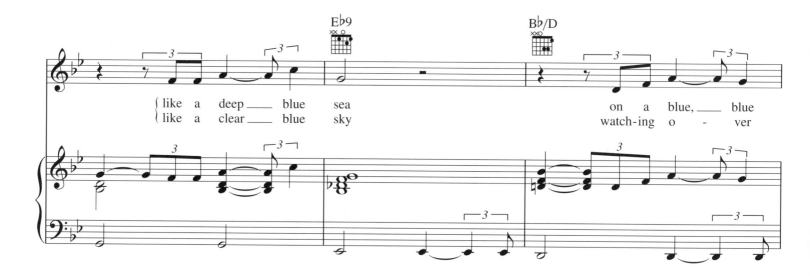

like a deep ___ blue sea
like a clear ___ blue sky

on a blue, ___ blue
watch-ing o - ver

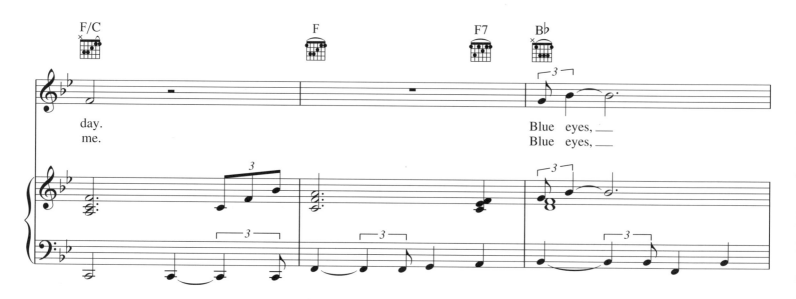

day.
me.

Blue eyes, ___
Blue eyes, ___

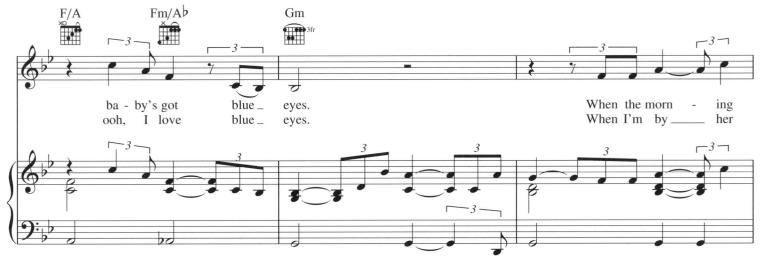

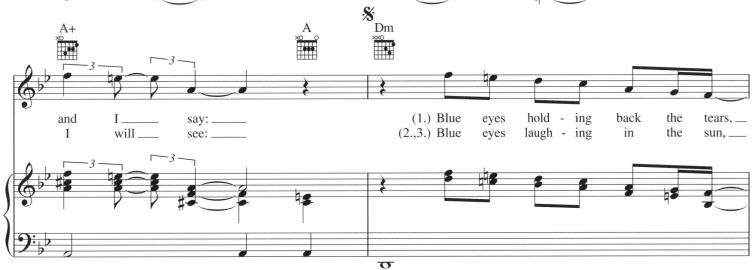

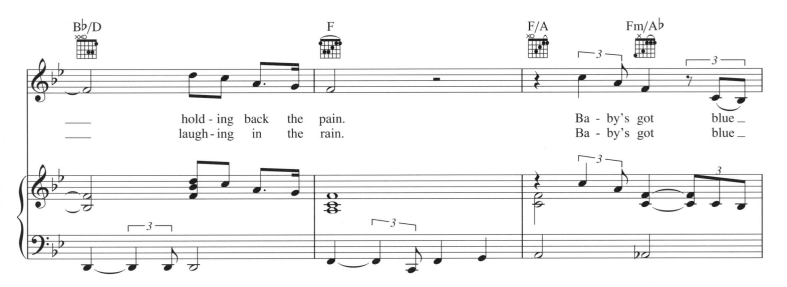

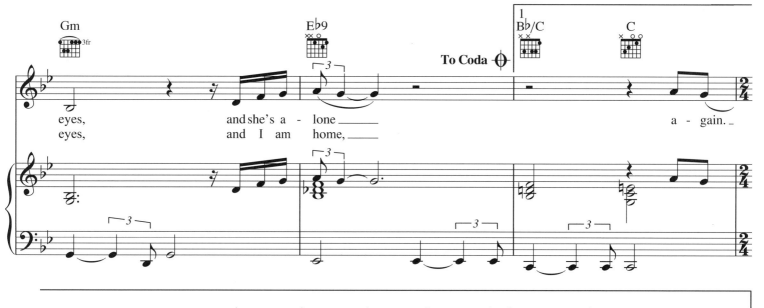

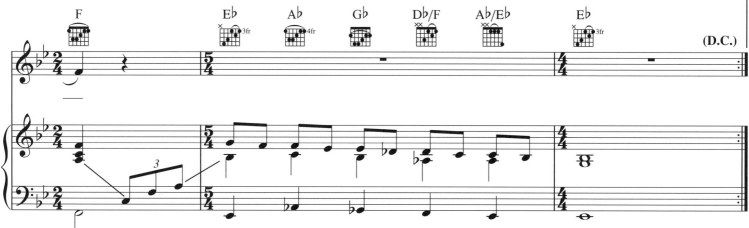

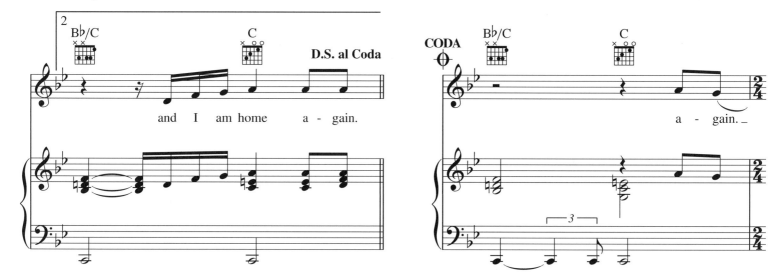

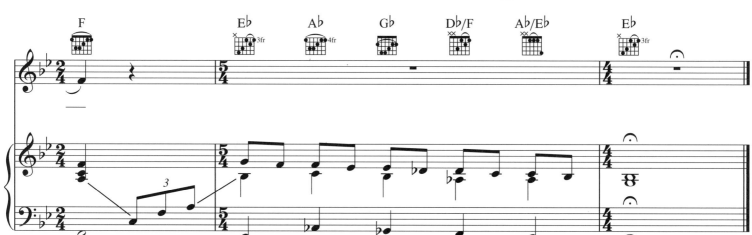

DON'T GO BREAKING MY HEART

Words and Music by CARTE BLANCHE
and ANN ORSON

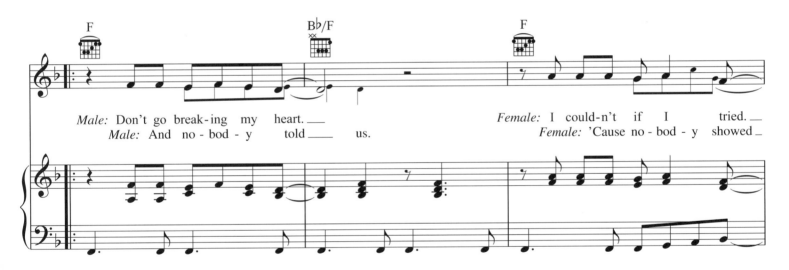

Male: Don't go break-ing my heart. ___
Male: And no-bod-y told ___ us.

Female: I could-n't if I tried. ___
Female: 'Cause no-bod-y showed ___

___ us.

Male: Oh, hon-ey, if I ___ get rest-less,
Male: And now ___ it's up ___ to us, ___ babe.

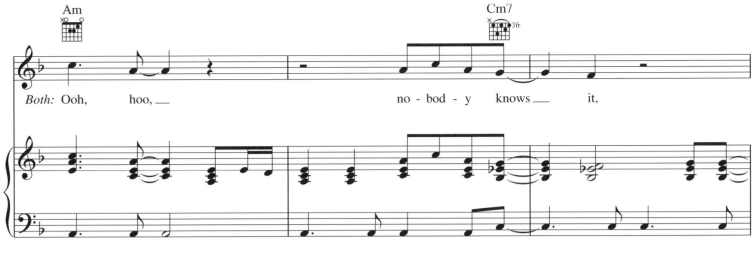

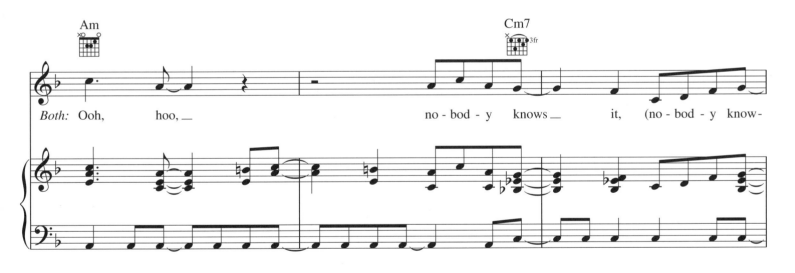

Oh, _____ oh, _____ I gave you my heart. _____

Male: So, don't go break-ing my heart. _____

To Coda ⊕

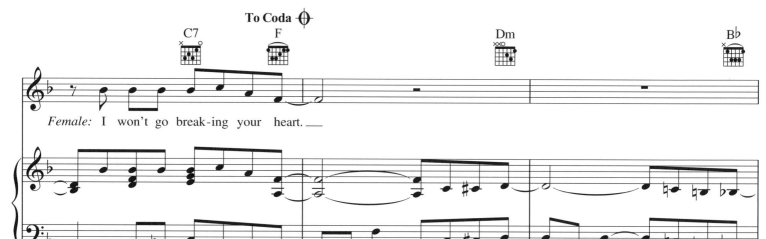

Female: I won't go break-ing your heart. __

Both: Don't go break-ing my heart. __

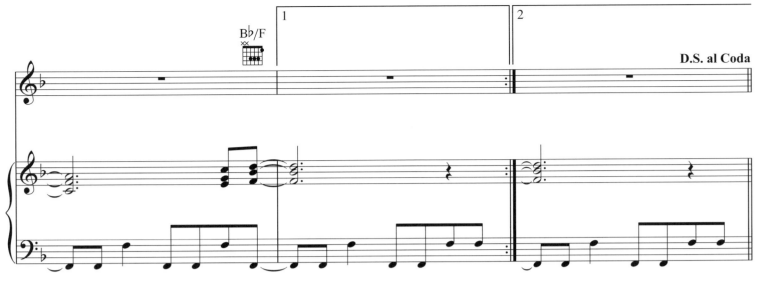

D.S. al Coda

Both:
___ Don't go break-ing my, don't go break-ing my, don't go break-ing my heart. _

Female:
I won't go break-ing your heart. _ don't go break-ing my heart. ___

CAN YOU FEEL THE LOVE TONIGHT

from Walt Disney Pictures' THE LION KING

Music by ELTON JOHN
Lyrics by TIM RICE

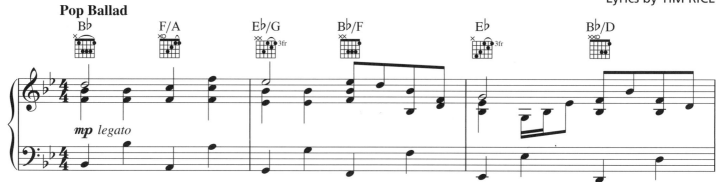

There's a calm _____ sur - ren - der
There's a time _____ for ev - 'ry - one,

to the rush _____ of day, _____ when the heat _____ of the roll - ing world _____
if they on - ly learn _____ that the twist - ing ka - lei - do - scope _____

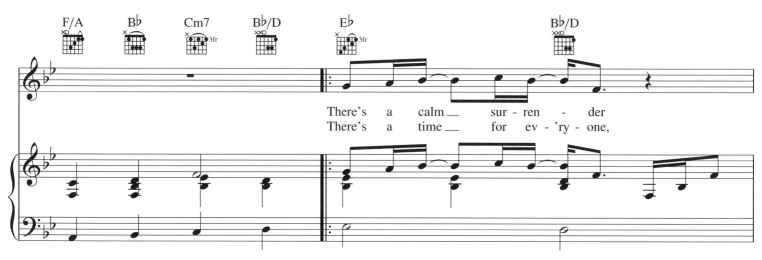

can be turned _____ a - way. _____ An en - chant - ed mo - ment,
moves us all _____ in turn. _____ There's a rhyme _____ and rea - son

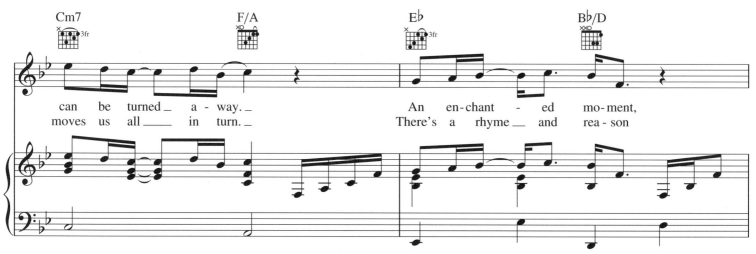

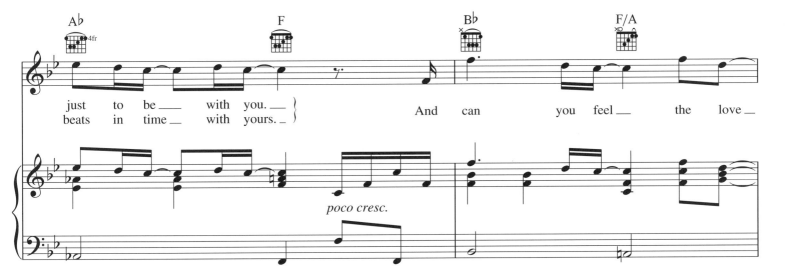

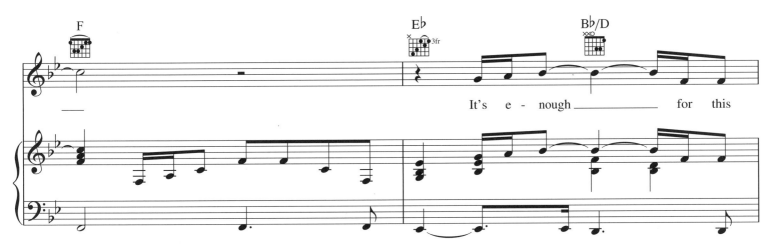

wide - eyed ___ wan - der - er   that we got this far. ___

___   And can you feel ___ the love ___

___ to - night, ___   how it's laid ___ to rest? ___

___   It's e - nough ___ to make

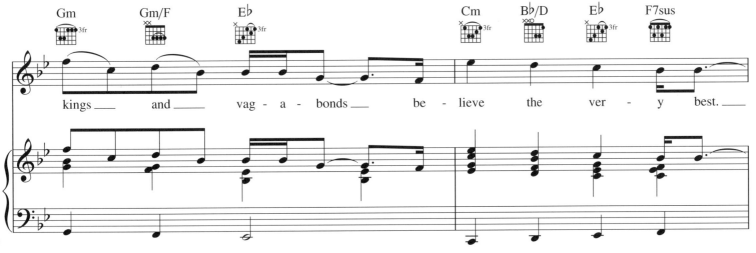

kings ___ and ___ vag-a-bonds ___ be - lieve the ver - y best. ___

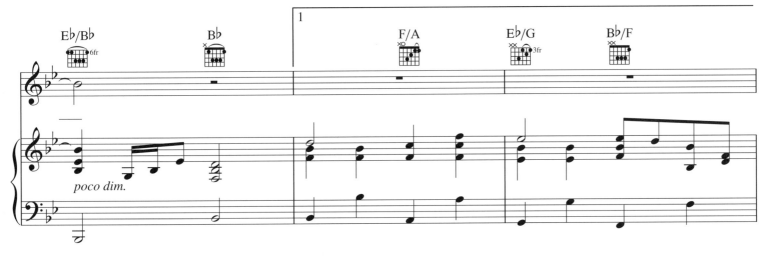

poco dim.

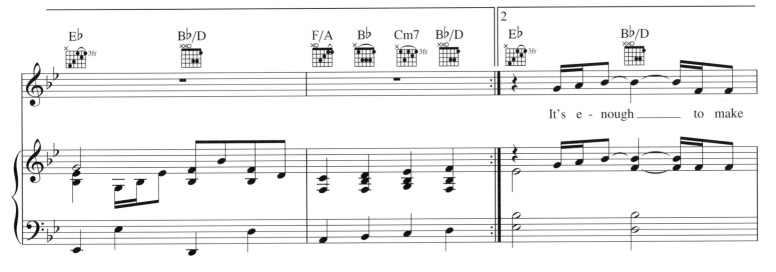

It's e - nough ___ to make

kings ___ and ___ vag-a-bonds ___ be - lieve the ver - y best. ___

molto rit.

CHLOE

Words and Music by ELTON JOHN
and GARY OSBORNE

How come you're ___ so un - der - stand -
How you han - dle what ___ you live ___
You're the life - line that ___ I cling ___

- in' _____
___ through _____
___ to _____

when I tell ___
I can nev -
when I feel ___

you more __ than ev - er, _____
you more __ than ev - er. _____
you more __ than ev - er, _____

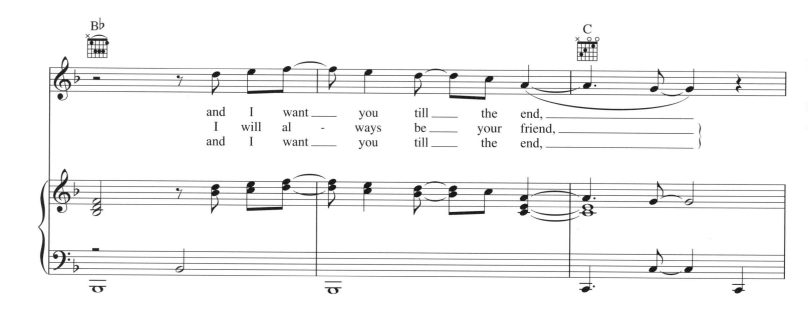

and I want ___ you till ___ the end, _____
I will al - ways be ___ your friend, _____
and I want ___ you till ___ the end, _____

Chlo - e. _____

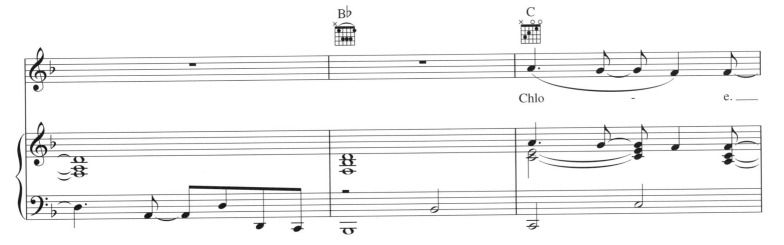

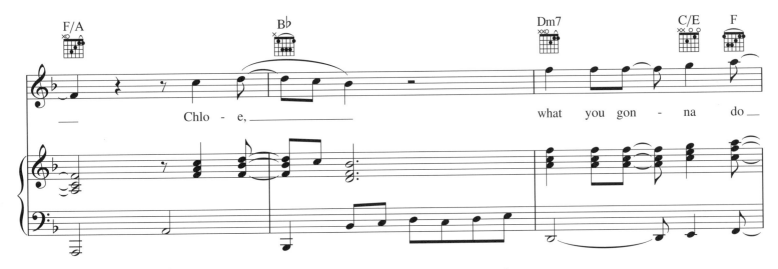

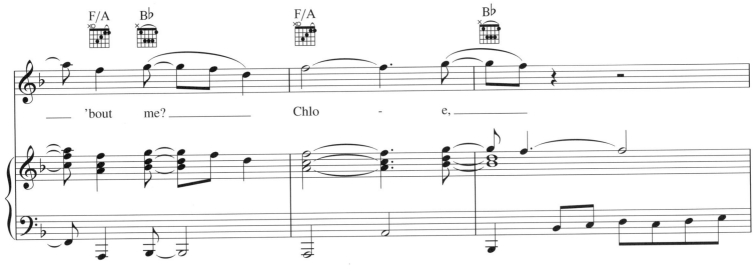

DON'T LET THE SUN GO DOWN ON ME

Words and Music by ELTON JOHN
and BERNIE TAUPIN

Moderately slow

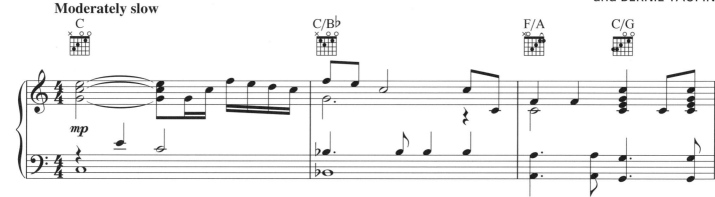

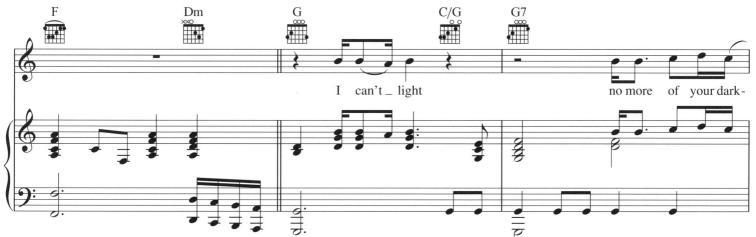

I can't _ light no more of your dark-

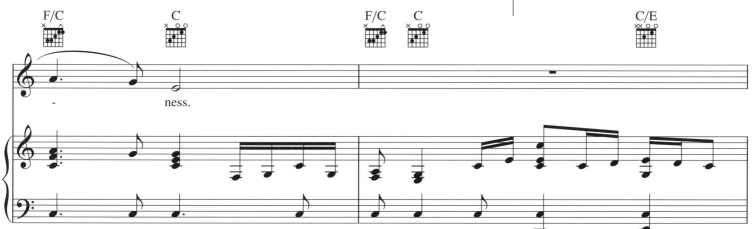

-ness.

All my pic-tures _____ seem to fade _ to black _ and white. _

Too late ___ to save my-self from fall - ing.

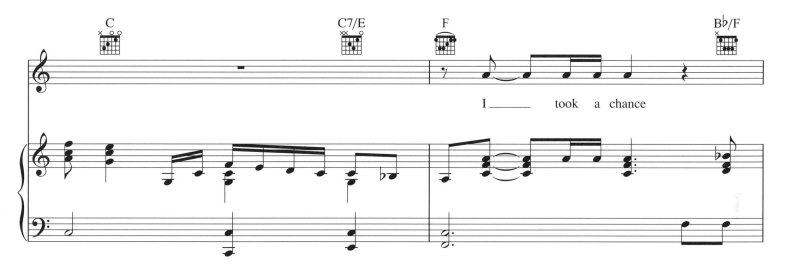

I _____ took a chance

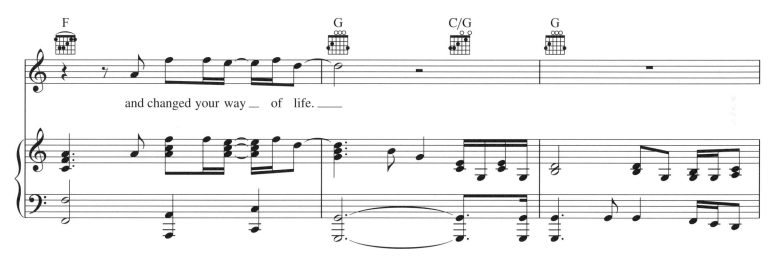

and changed your way __ of life. ___

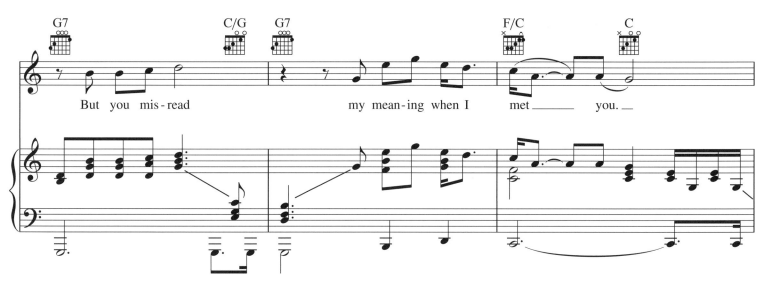

But you mis-read my mean-ing when I met _____ you. __

Closed the door and left me blind-

-ed by the light.

Don't let the sun go down on me.

Al-though I search my-self, it's al-ways some-one else I see.

I'd just al - low a frag - ment of your life _____ to wan - der free. _____

_____ But

los - ing ev - 'ry - thing _____ is like the sun go - ing down on _____

To Coda

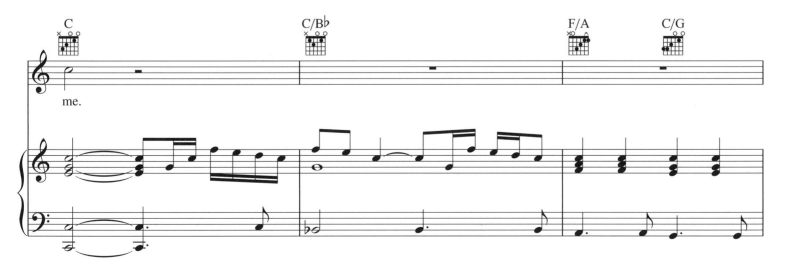

me.

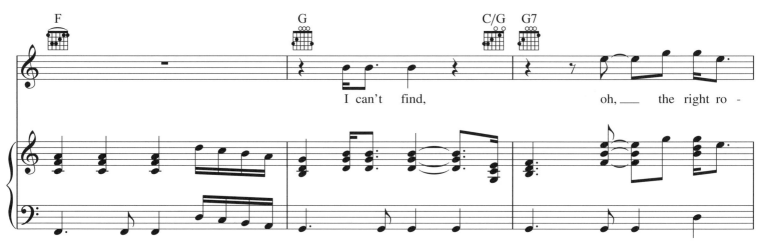

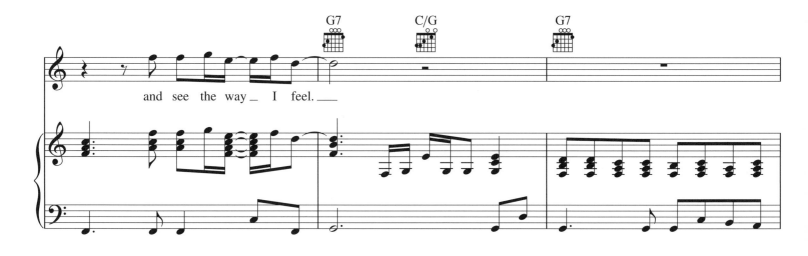

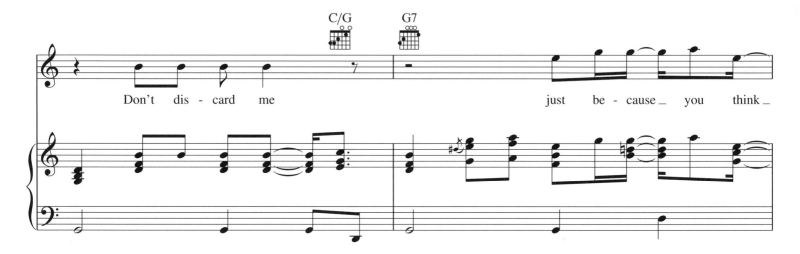

I mean _ you harm. _____

But these cuts _ I ____ have, _____ oh, they need love _____ to help _ them

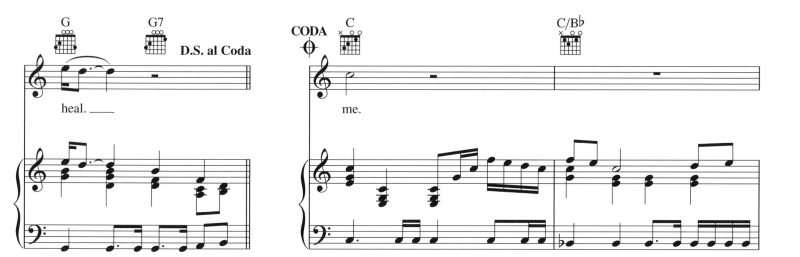

D.S. al Coda

heal. ____

CODA

me.

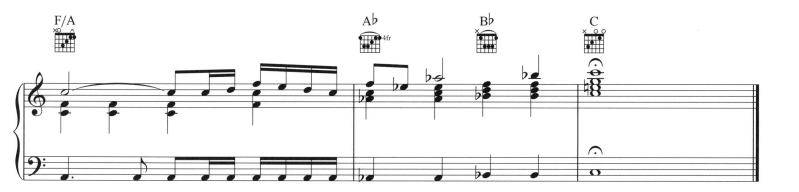

I GUESS THAT'S WHY THEY CALL IT THE BLUES

Words and Music by ELTON JOHN,
BERNIE TAUPIN and DAVEY JOHNSTONE

run ___ to the place in ___ our hearts ___ where ___ we hide. ___

you ___ more than ___ I love ___ life ___ it - self. ___

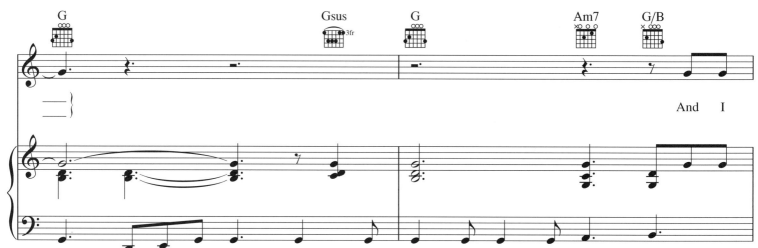

___ And I

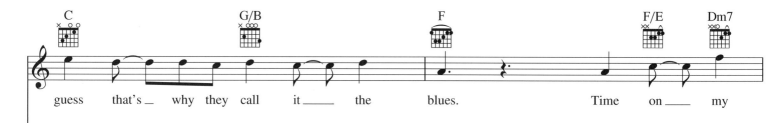

guess that's ___ why they call it ___ the blues. Time on ___ my

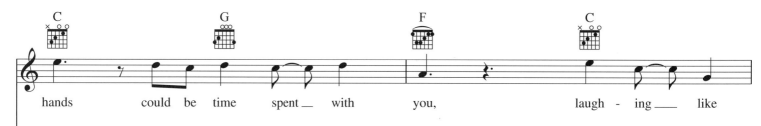

hands could be time spent ___ with you, laugh - ing ___ like

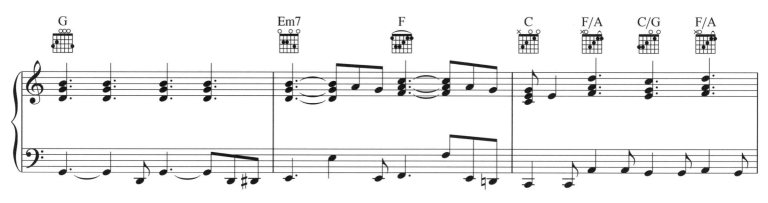

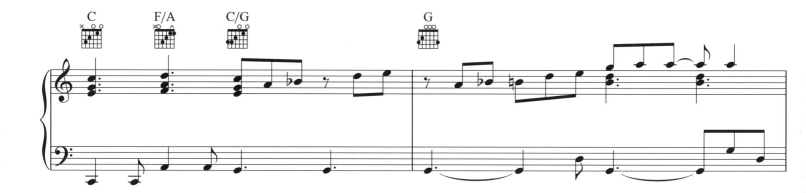

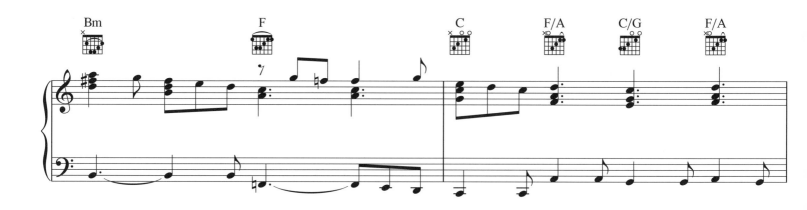

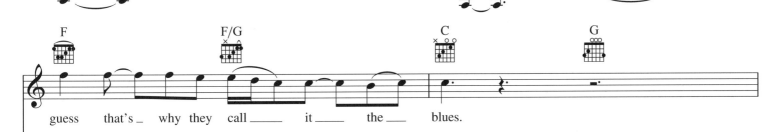

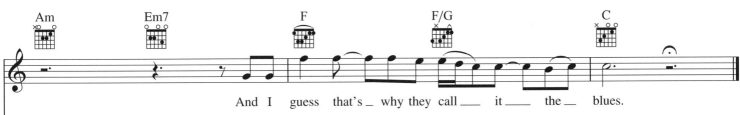

I WANT LOVE

Words and Music by ELTON JOHN
and BERNIE TAUPIN

Slowly, evenly

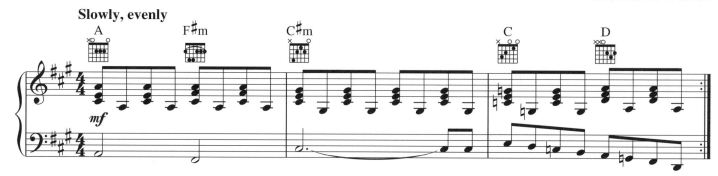

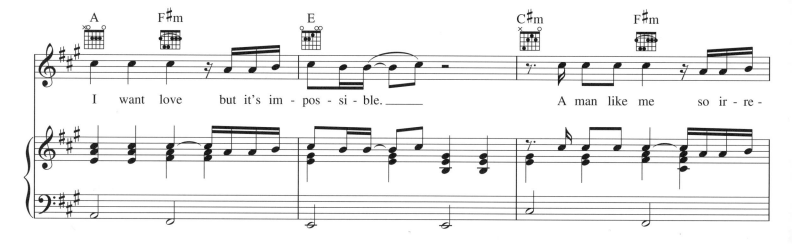

I want love but it's im-pos-si-ble. A man like me so ir-re-

spon-si-ble. A man like me is dead in plac-es

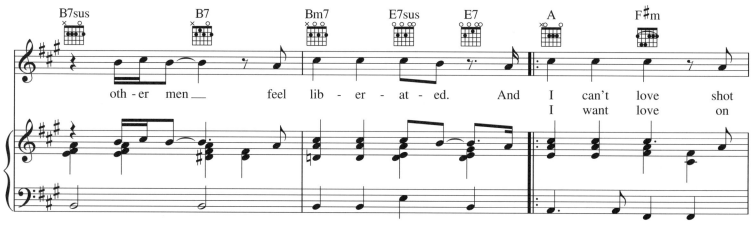

oth-er men ___ feel lib-er-at-ed. And I can't love shot
I want love on

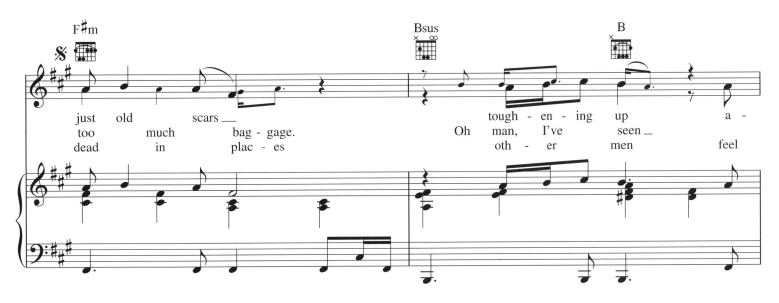

I want love, won't break me down, won't break me up, won't fence me in. I want a

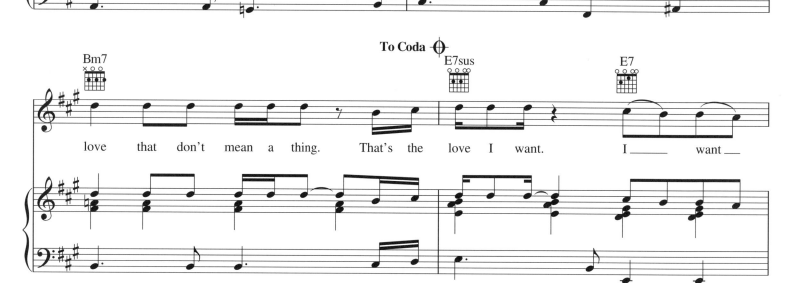

love that don't mean a thing. That's the love I want. I___ want ___

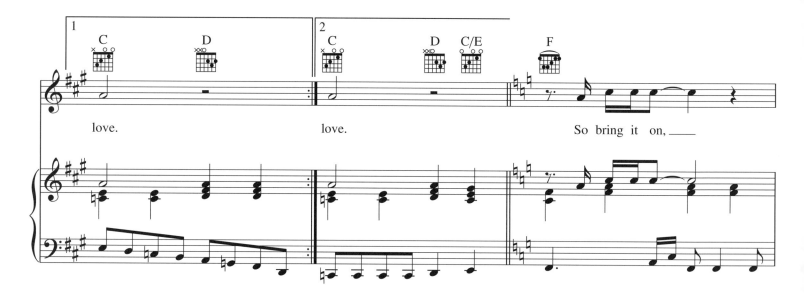

love. love. So bring it on, ___

I've ___ been bruised. ___ Don't give me love that's clean ___ and smooth. ___

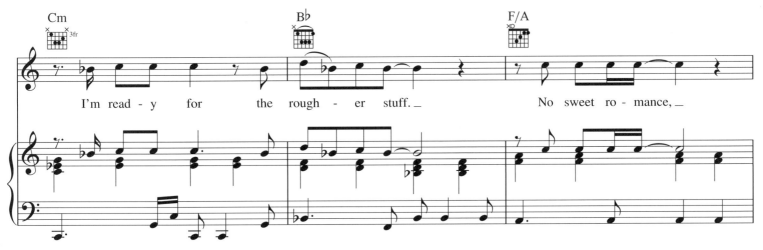

I'm read-y for the rough-er stuff. __ No sweet ro-mance, __

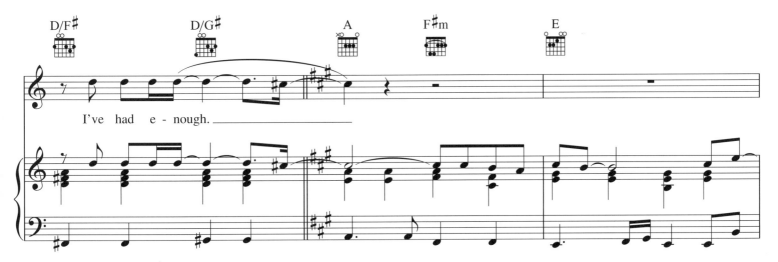

I've had e-nough. _____

A man like me is

D.S. al Coda

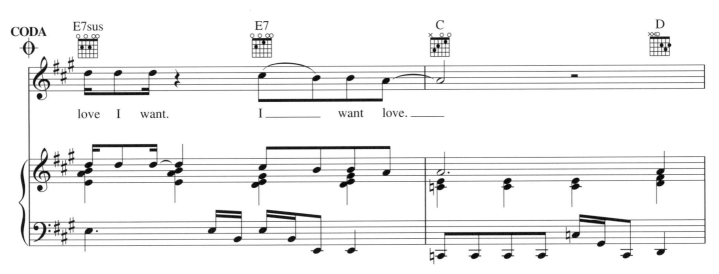

love I want. I _____ want love. _____

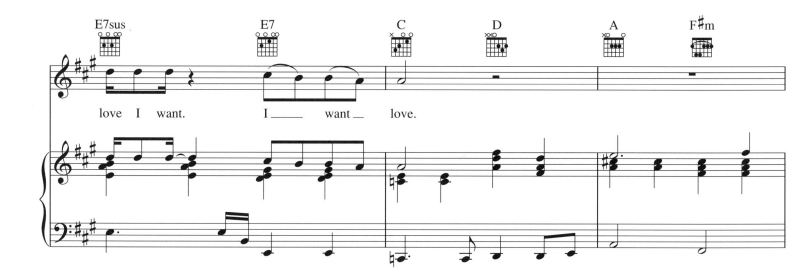

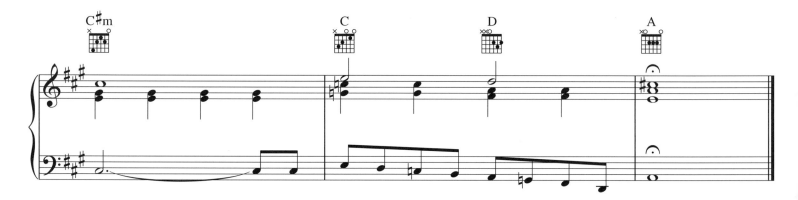

I'VE BEEN LOVING YOU

Words and Music by ELTON JOHN
and BERNIE TAUPIN

Moderately

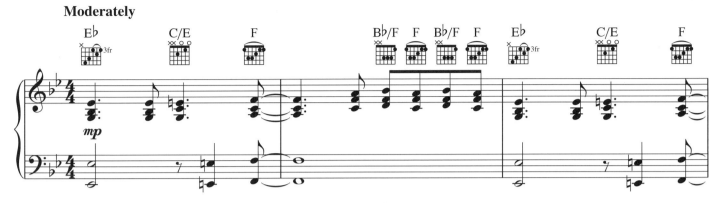

I _____ did-n't mean to _____
So _____ don't _____ you _____

_____ hurt you; _____ you know _____ it's just
_____ feel sad; _____ it's not _____ the thing

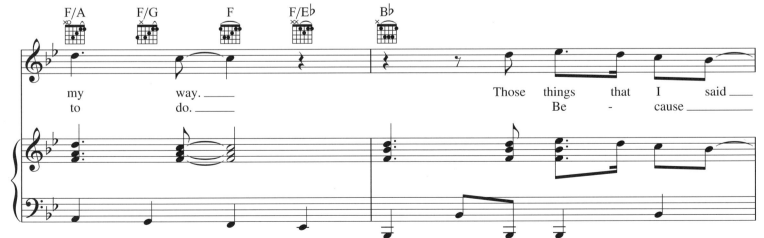

my _____ way. _____ Those things that I said _____
to do. _____ Be - cause _____

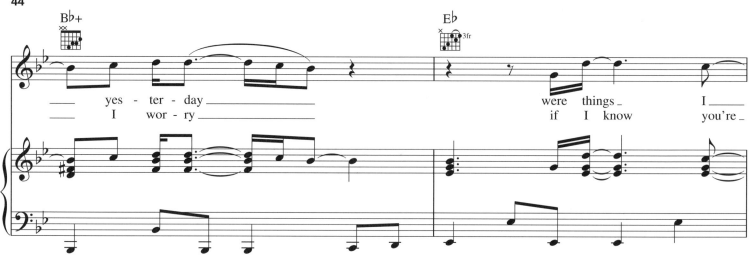

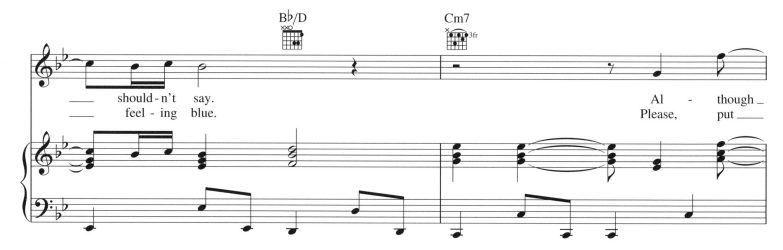

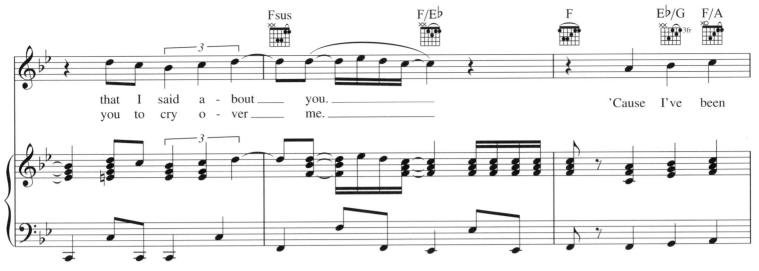

that I said a-bout ____ you. ____ 'Cause I've been
you to cry o-ver ____ me. ____

lov-ing you, ba—by, lov-ing you, ba—by, for a long time. _

And if you go a-way, _ I just won't know _ what _ to do. _

Yes, I've been lov-ing you, ba—by,

lov - ing you, ba - by, for a long time. ___ And you

know in your heart that I'll al - ways wor - ship you. ___

1

I could - n't bear to see you go. ___ Oh,

no, no, no, no. ___ 'Cause I've been

loving you, baby, loving you, baby, for a long time.

And if you go away, I just won't know what to do.

Repeat and Fade **Optional Ending**

'Cause I've been

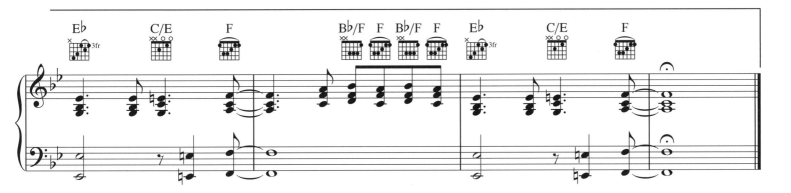

IT'S ME THAT YOU NEED

Words and Music by ELTON JOHN
and BERNIE TAUPIN

With motion

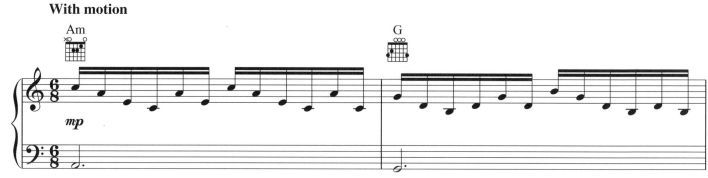

Hey there, look in the mir-

-ror.

Are you a-fraid _____ you might see me _____ look-ing at

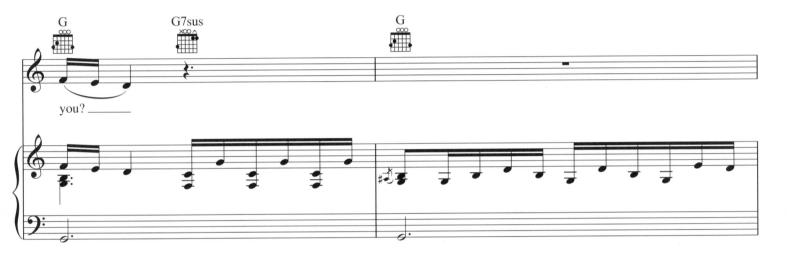

you? _____

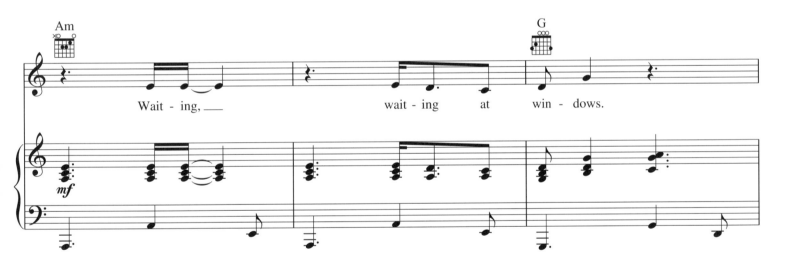

Wait - ing, _____ wait - ing at win - dows.

Oh, it's me that you need, _____ yes it's me, _____

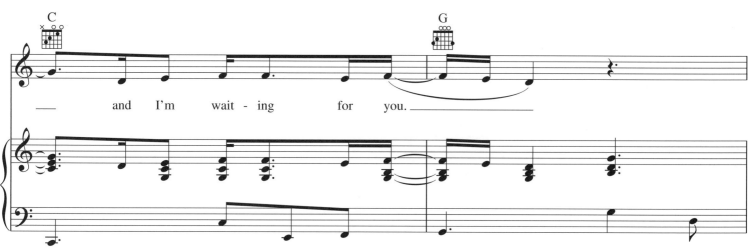

and I'm wait - ing for you. _____

But I re - main si - lent.

Oh, I won't say a word. _____ I'll leave you _ to

re - a - lize I'm the light _____ in your world. ___ And it's

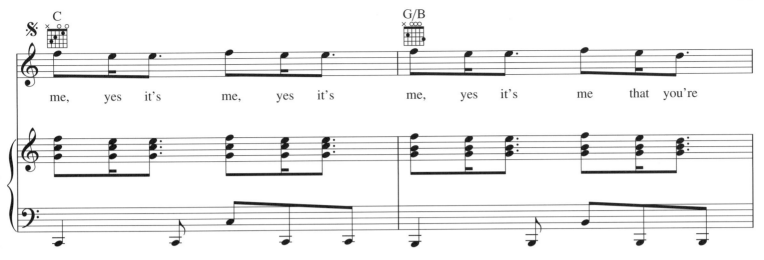

me, yes it's   me, yes it's   me, yes it's   me that you're

need - ing.   It's

me, yes it's   me, yes it's   me,____ yes it's   me ____ that you need. _

Yes it's

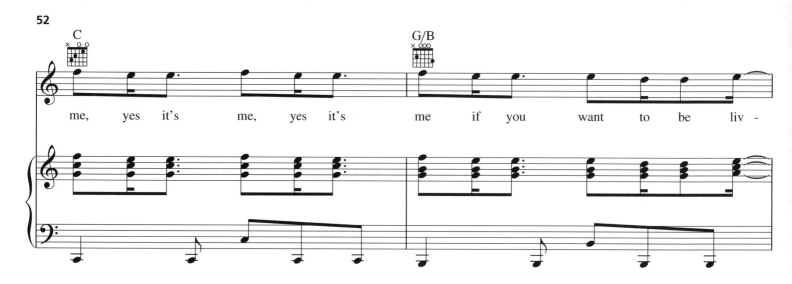

me, yes it's me, yes it's me if you want to be liv-

- ing. I'm the one ___

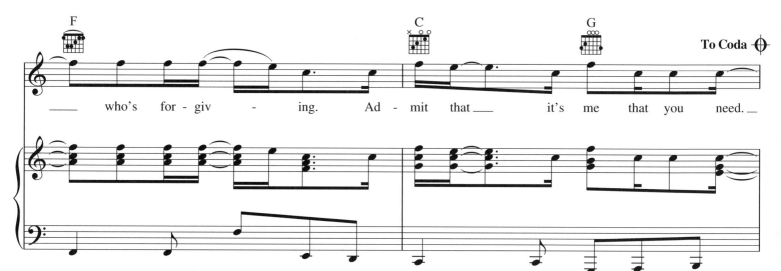

___ who's for-giv - ing. Ad - mit that ___ it's me that you need. ___

To Coda ⊕

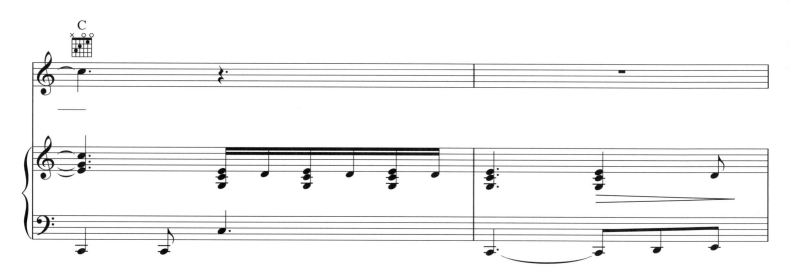

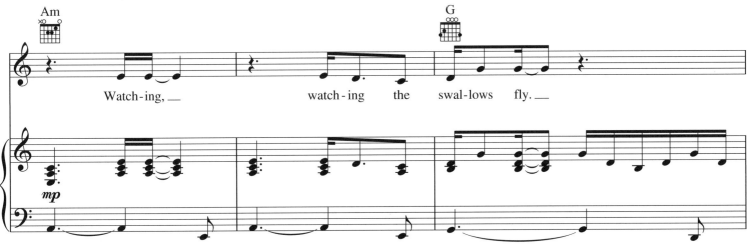

Watch-ing, ___ watch-ing the swal-lows fly. ___

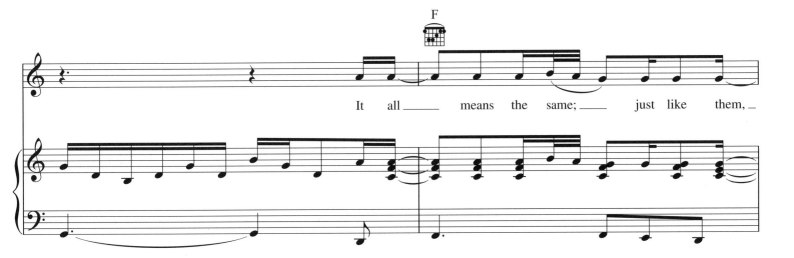

It all ___ means the same; ___ just like them, ___

___ you can fly home a - gain. ___

But don't, no, don't for - get yes - ter - day.

Pride is an ug - ly word, girl, ____ and you still know my

name. ___ But I ____ re - main si -

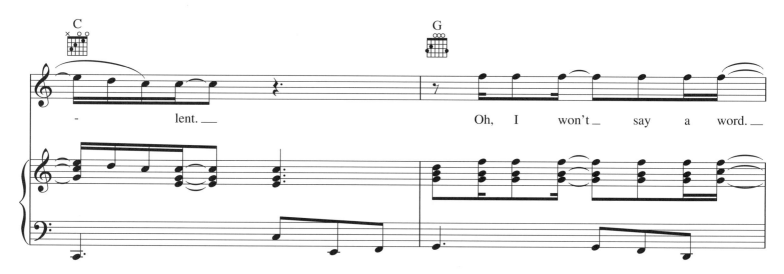

- lent. ___ Oh, I won't _ say a word. ___

_____ I'll leave you to re -

- a - lize _____ I'm the light _____ in your world. __ And it's

CODA

I'm the one __

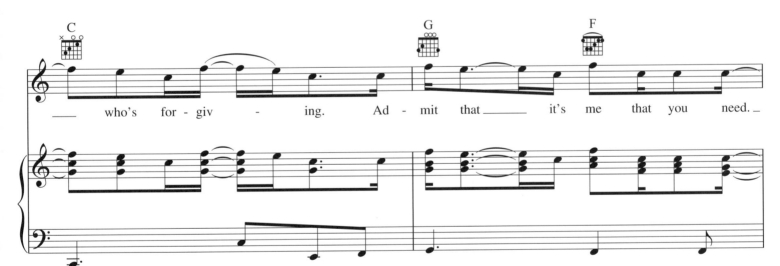

__ who's for - giv - ing. Ad - mit that _____ it's me that you need. __

Oh. _____ I'm the one __

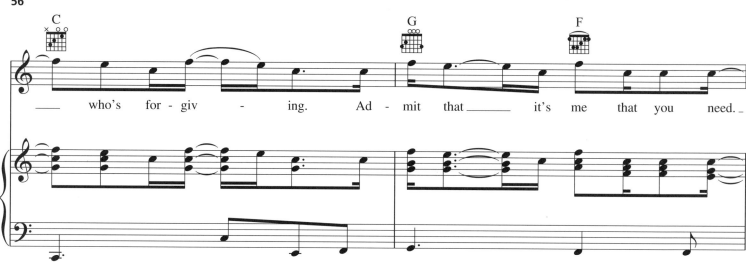

who's for - giv - ing. Ad - mit that _____ it's me that you need. _

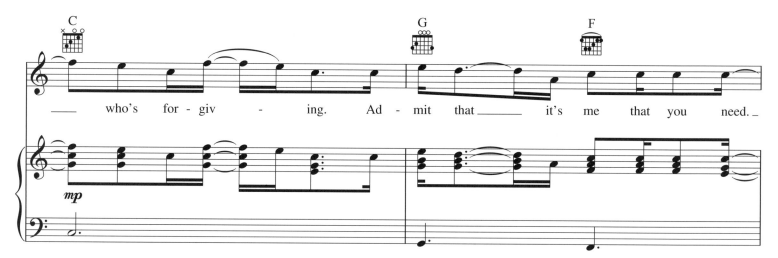

_____ Oh. _____ Well, I'm the one _

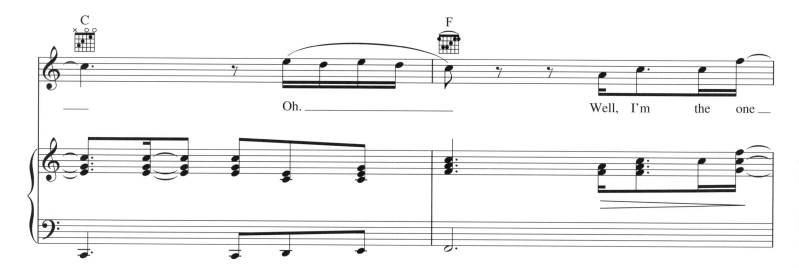

_____ who's for - giv - ing. Ad - mit that _____ it's me that you need. _

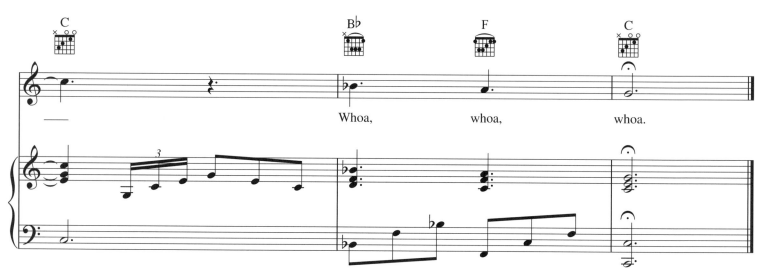

_____ Whoa, whoa, whoa.

LOVE LIES BLEEDING

By ELTON JOHN
and BERNIE TAUPIN

Driving Rock

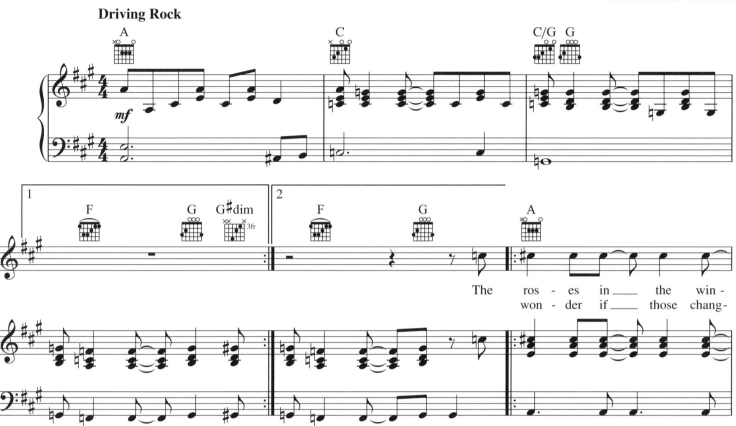

The ros - es in ____ the win -
won - der if ____ those chang -

- dow box ____ have tilt - ed to one side. _____
- es have left a scar on you, _____

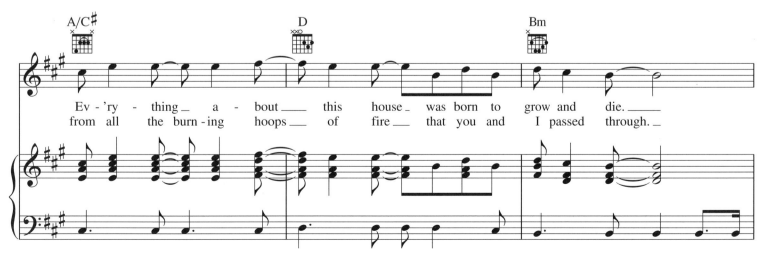

Ev - 'ry - thing ____ a - bout ____ this house ____ was born to grow and die. ____
from all the burn - ing hoops ____ of fire ___ that you and I passed through. ____

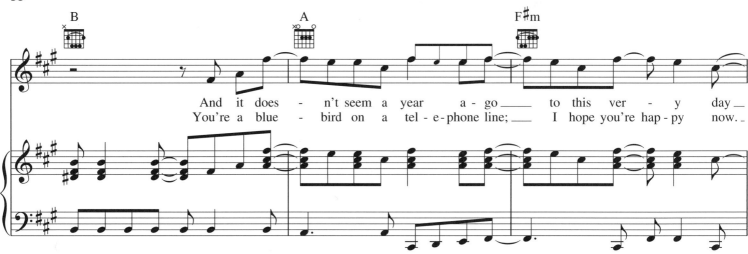

And it does - n't seem a year a - go____ to this ver - y day____
You're a blue - bird on a tel - e - phone line; ____ I hope you're hap - py now.__

you said, "I'm sor - ry, hon - ey. If I
Well, if the wind of change __ comes down, __

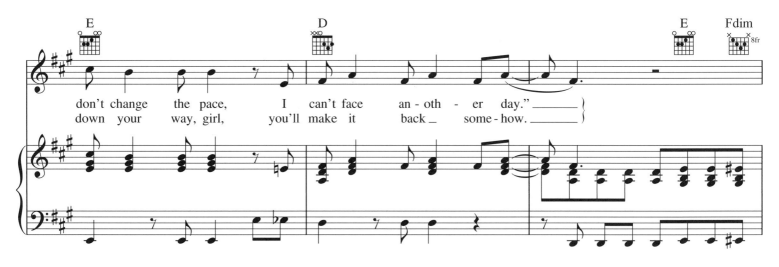

don't change the pace, I can't face an - oth - er day." ____
down your way, girl, you'll make it back __ some - how. ____

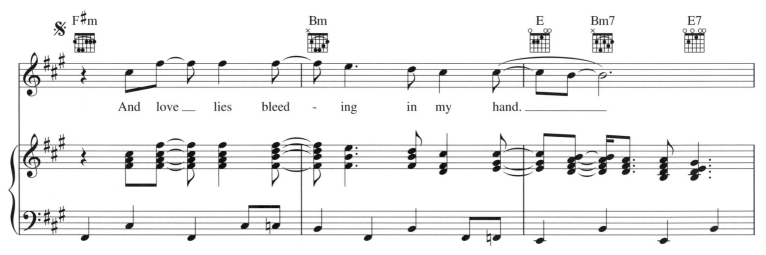

And love __ lies bleed - ing in my hand. ____

Oh, it kills me to think __ of you __ with an - oth - er man. __

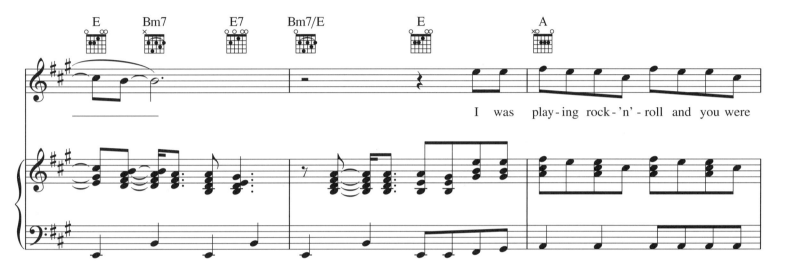

__ I was play-ing rock-'n'-roll and you were

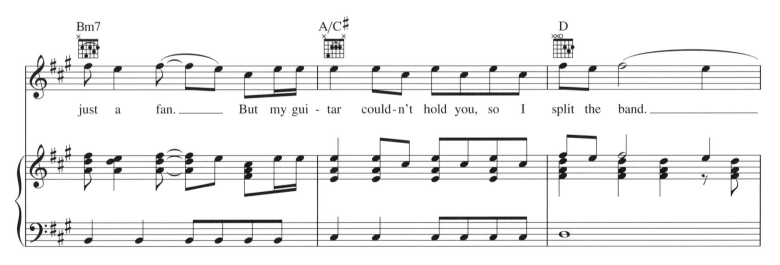

just a fan. ____ But my gui - tar could-n't hold you, so I split the band. ____

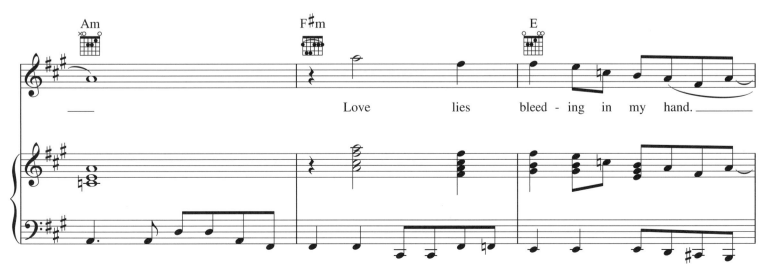

Love lies bleed-ing in my hand. ____

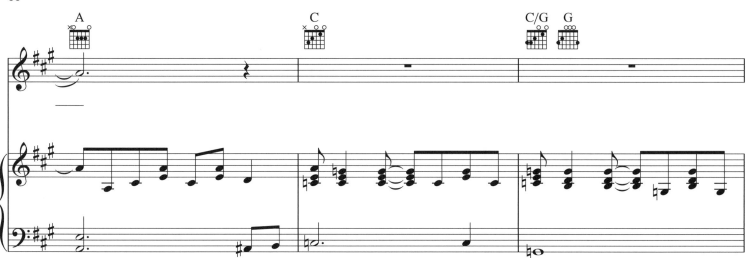

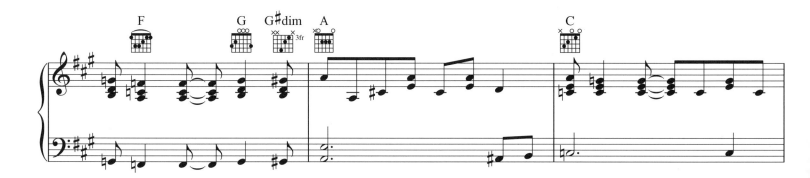

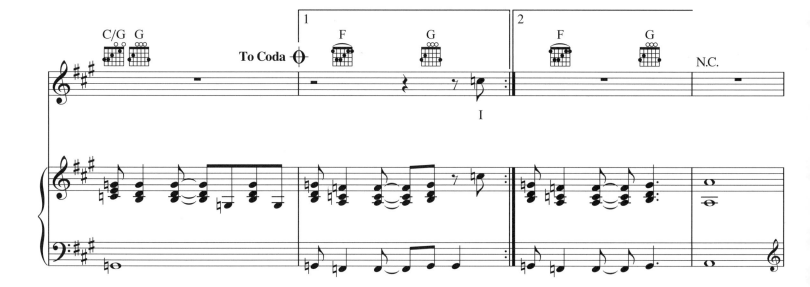

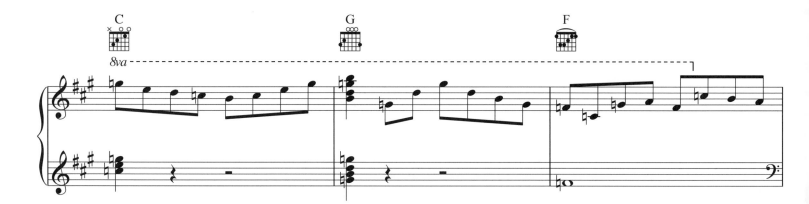

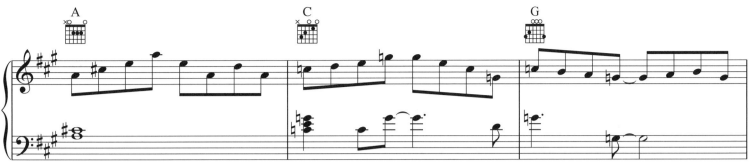

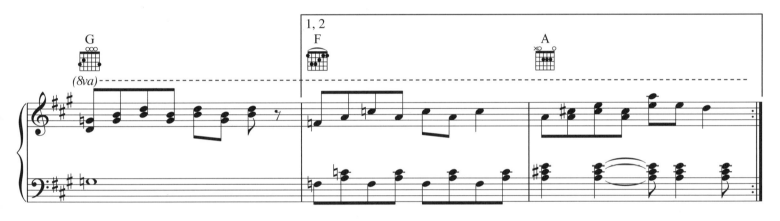

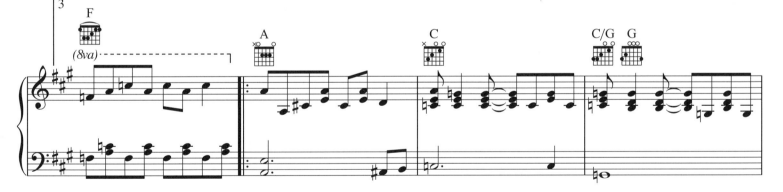

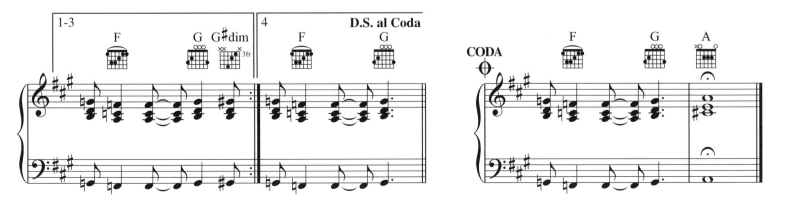

LITTLE JEANNIE

Words and Music by ELTON JOHN
and GARY OSBORNE

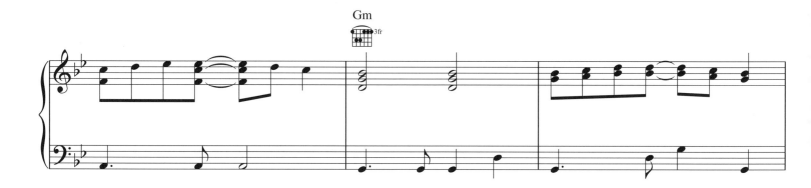

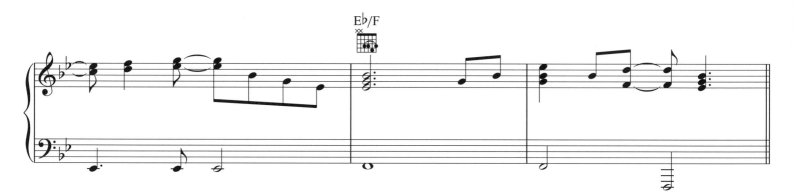

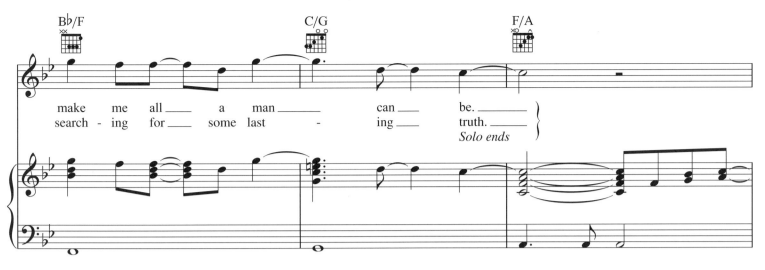

make me all ___ a man ___ can ___ be. ___
search - ing for ___ some last - ing ___ truth. ___

Solo ends

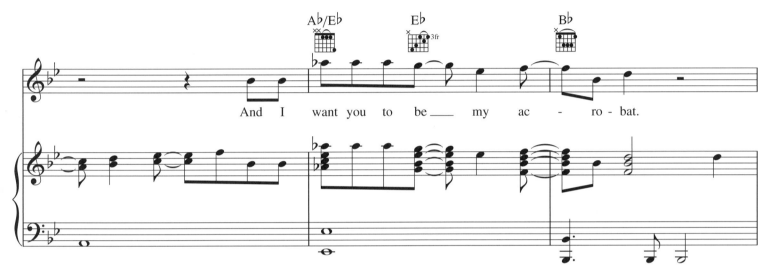

And I want you to be ___ my ac - ro - bat.

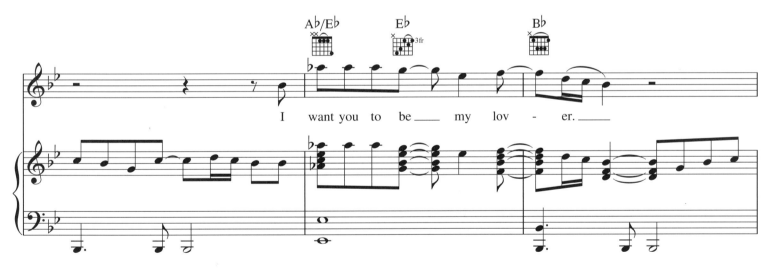

I want you to be ___ my lov - er. ___

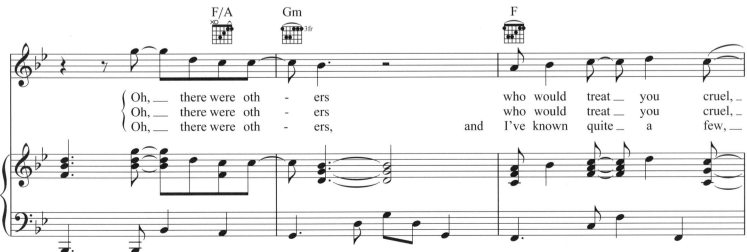

Oh, ___ there were oth - ers   who would treat ___ you cruel, ___
Oh, ___ there were oth - ers   who would treat ___ you cruel, ___
Oh, ___ there were oth - ers,   and I've known quite a few, ___

and oh, _____ Jean - nie, _
but oh, _____ Jean - nie, _
but oh, _____ Jean - nie, _

you were al - ways some - one's fool.

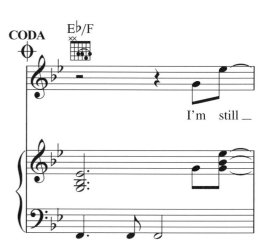

I'm still _

2

I will al - ways be __ your fool.

D.S. al Coda

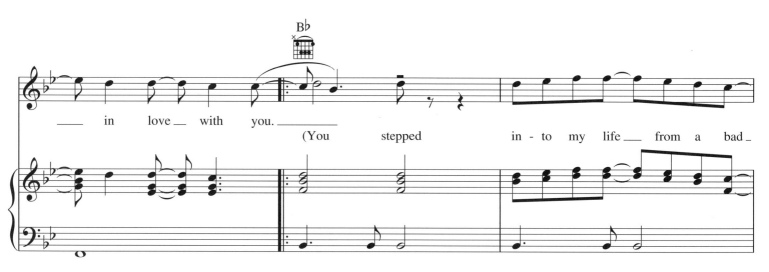

__ in love __ with you. _____ (You stepped in - to my life __ from a bad _

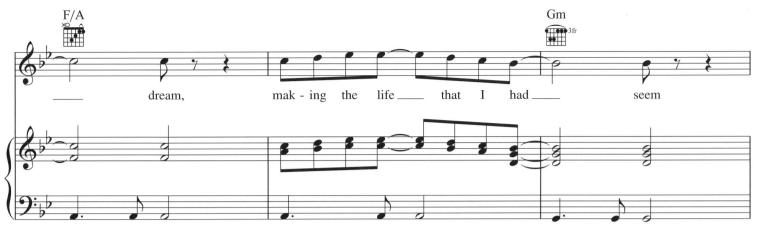

dream,   mak - ing the life ____ that I had ____ seem

sud - den - ly shin - y and new.) ____   Oh, Jean -

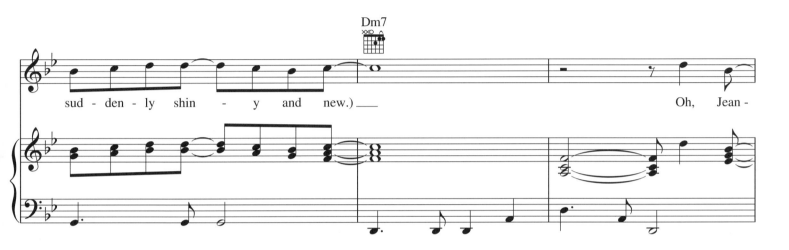

- nie, ____   I'm so ____

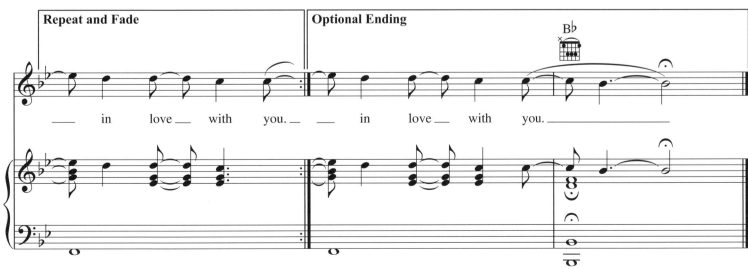

Repeat and Fade   **Optional Ending**

____ in love ____ with you. ____   ____ in love ____ with you. ____

MADE FOR ME

Words and Music by ELTON JOHN
and BERNIE TAUPIN

With a steady beat

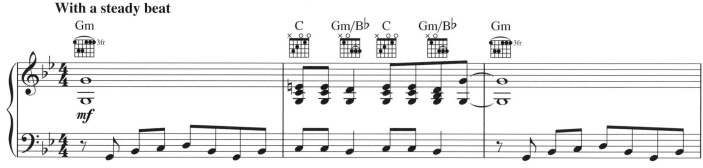

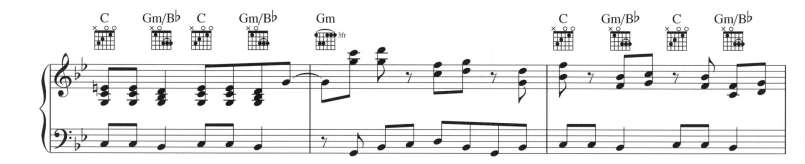

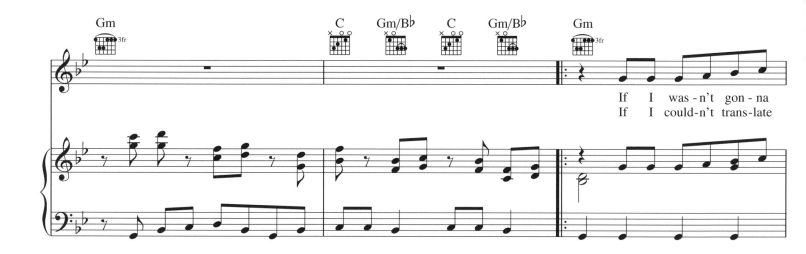

If I was-n't gon-na
If I could-n't trans-late

love you,   why was I born at all?___
fan-ta-sy,   oh,___   i-mag-ine how I'd feel.___

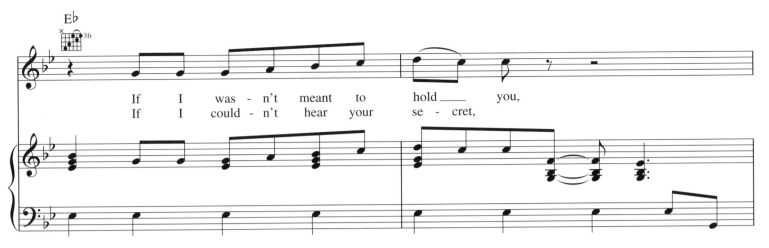

If I was-n't meant to hold _____ you,
If I could-n't hear your se - cret,

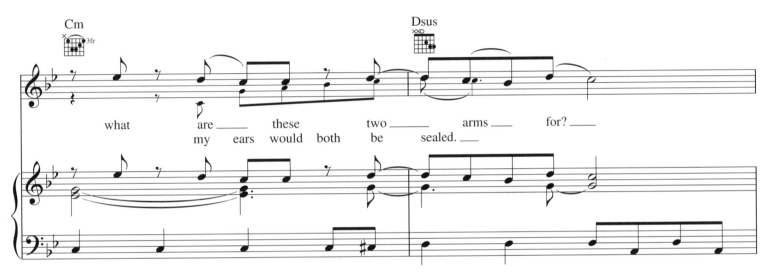

what are _____ these two _____ arms _____ for? _____
my ears would both be sealed. _____

If I can't pro - tect you,
If I can't make love _____ to you,

what are these mus-cles for? _
this bod - y has no

_____ And if I can't en - rich your _ life, _
use. _ If you be-lieved I loved you,

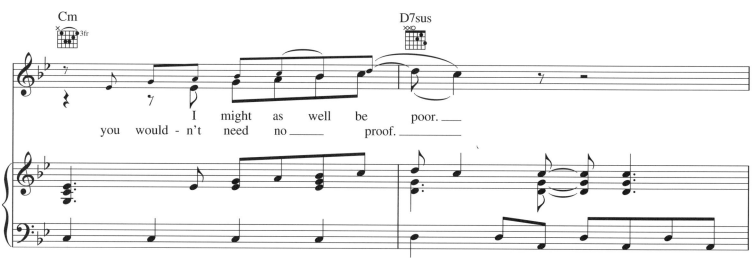

I might as well be poor. ___
you would-n't need no ___ proof. ___

If I could-n't see you na-ked, whoa, ___
And if I can't re-turn to you, oh, ___

___ I might as well be blind. ___
___ I would-n't need ___ my legs to run. ___

If I could-n't treat you right, ___
And if I can draw warmth ___ from you,

would-n't I be so _____ un-kind? _____ You were made for me. _____
why do ___ I need _____ the sun? _____

You were made for me. _____

You weren't born to be _____ a-lone, and you were made for me. _____

You were made for me. _____

You were made for me. _____ Flesh and bone, _ etched _

_____ in stone, _ you _____ were made for me. _

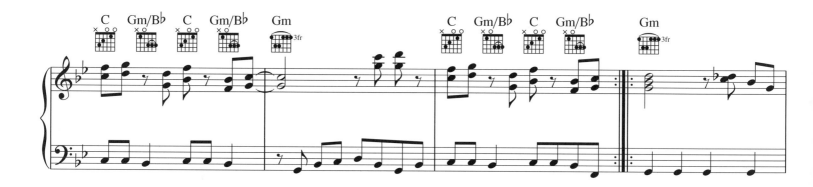

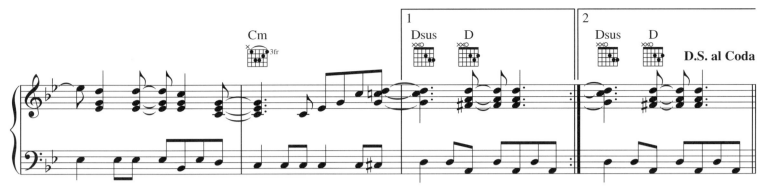

Made for me. _____

Made for me. ____

_____

You weren't born to be _____ a-lone, and

you were made for me. _____

MICHELLE'S SONG
from the Motion Picture FRIENDS

Words and Music by ELTON JOHN
and BERNIE TAUPIN

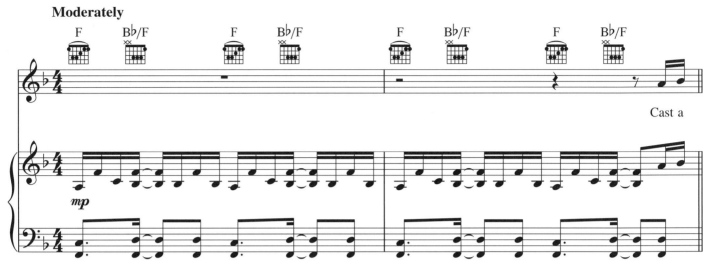

Cast a

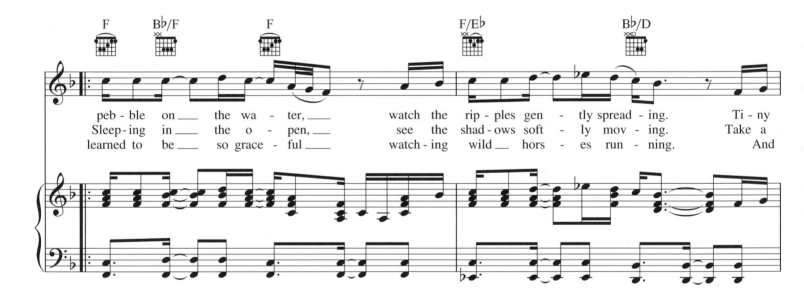

peb - ble on ___ the wa - ter, ___ watch the rip - ples gen - tly spread - ing. Ti - ny
Sleep - ing in ___ the o - pen, ___ see the shad - ows soft - ly mov - ing. Take a
learned to be ___ so grace - ful watch - ing wild ___ hors - es run - ning. And

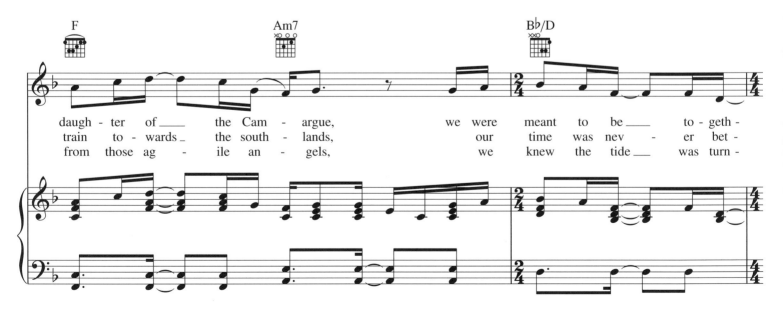

daugh - ter of ___ the Cam - argue, we were meant to be ___ to - geth -
train to - wards ___ the south - lands, our time was nev - er bet -
from those ag - ile an - gels, we knew the tide ___ was turn -

- -er. _____ We were made for one an-oth-er _____ in a
- -ter. _____ We shall pass the sights of splen-dor _____ on the
- -ing. _____ For we watched as on the sky-way _____ the

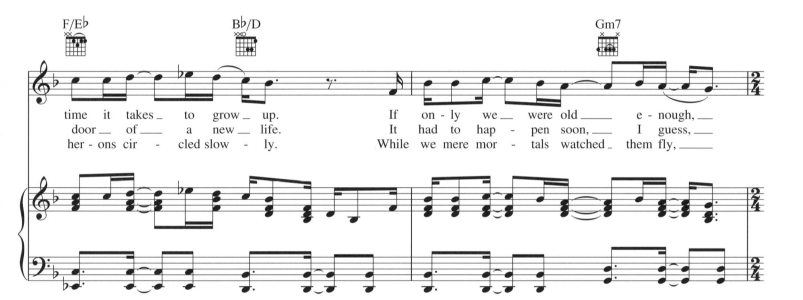

time it takes _ to grow _ up. If on-ly we _ were old _____ e-nough, _
door _ of _ a new _ life. It had to hap-pen soon, ___ I guess, _
her-ons cir-cled slow-ly. While we mere mor-tals watched _ them fly, _____

then they _____ might leave _____ us both _ a-lone.
wheth-er _____ it is wrong _____ or it _____ is right.
our sleep-less eyes _____ grew _ heav-y. _____

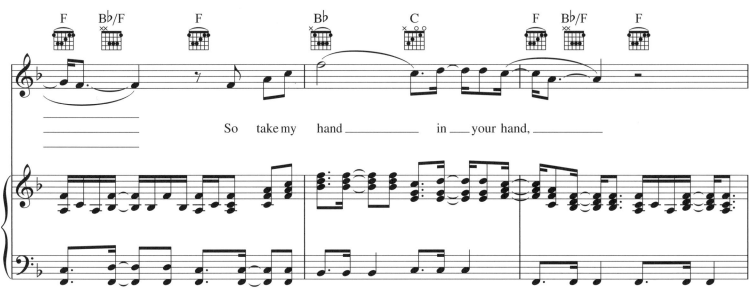

So take my hand _____ in ___ your hand, _____

say it's great _ to be ___ a - live. _____ No one's

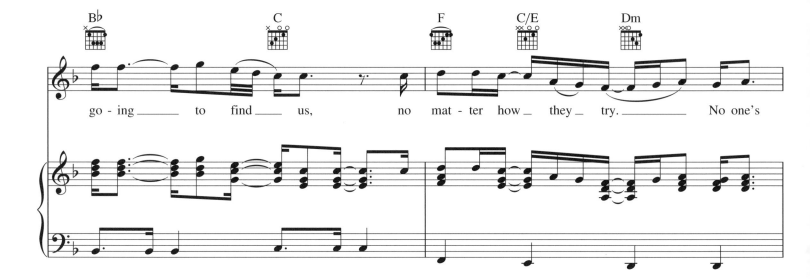

go - ing _____ to find ___ us, no mat - ter how_ they _ try. _____ No one's

go - ing _ to find ___ us. It's won-der-ful, ___ so wild ___ be-neath the sky. _

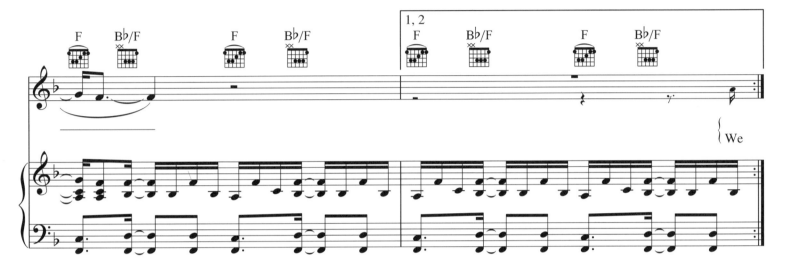

We

So take my __ hand _____ in ___ your hand, _

say it's great _ to be _ a - live. _

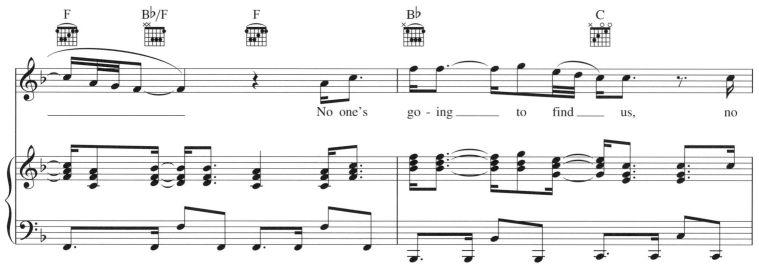

No one's go-ing ___ to find ___ us, no

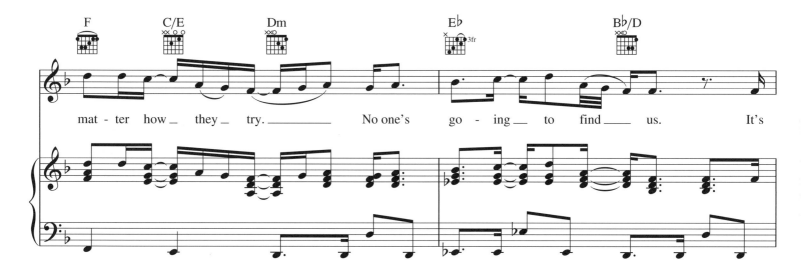

mat-ter how ___ they ___ try. ___ No one's go-ing ___ to find ___ us. It's

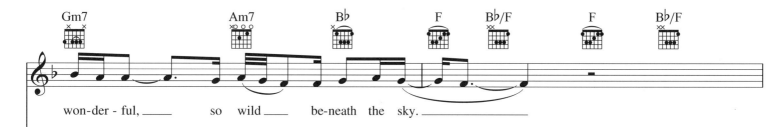

won-der-ful, ___ so wild ___ be-neath the sky. ___

NIKITA

Words and Music by ELTON JOHN
and BERNIE TAUPIN

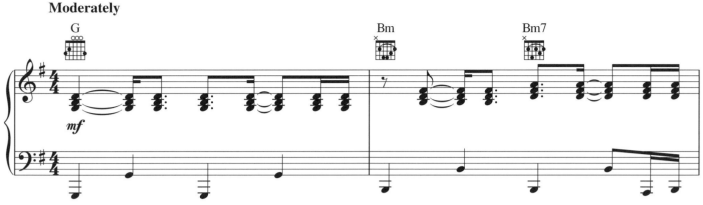

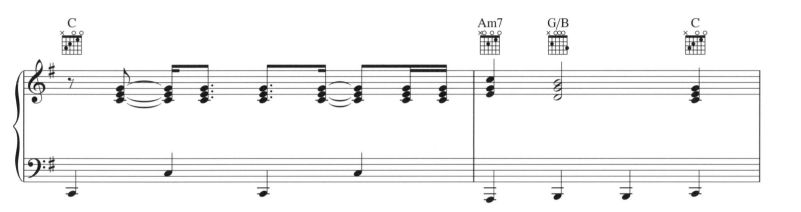

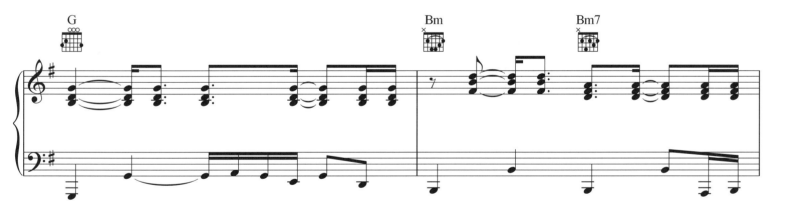

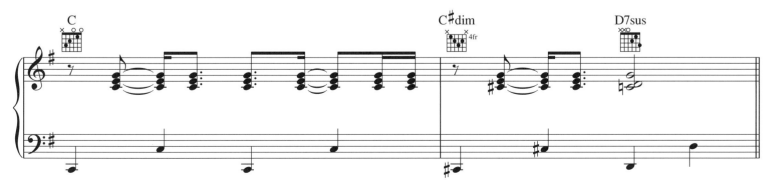

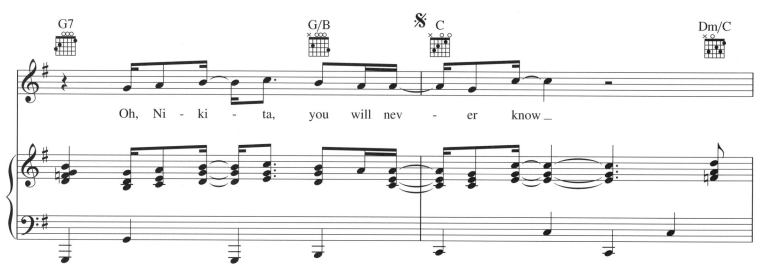

Oh, Ni - ki - ta, you will nev - er know __

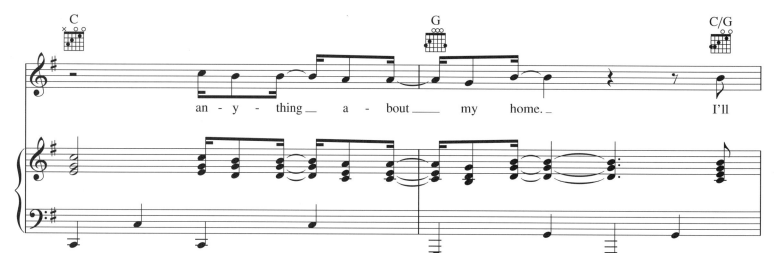

an - y - thing __ a - bout __ my home. __ I'll

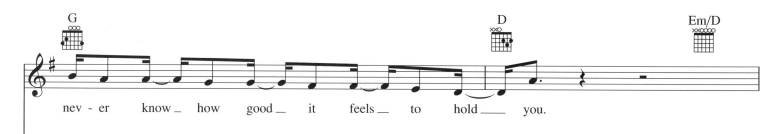

nev - er know __ how good __ it feels __ to hold __ you.

Ni - ki - ta, __ I need you __ so. Oh, Ni - ki - ta, is __ the

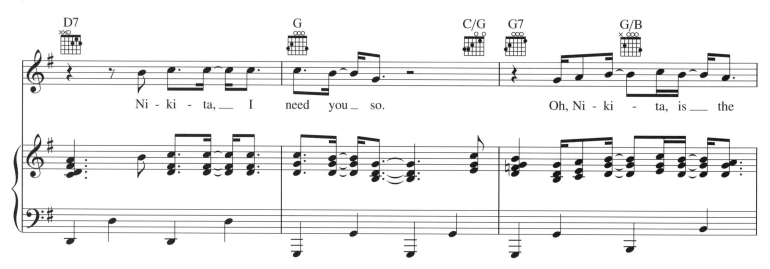

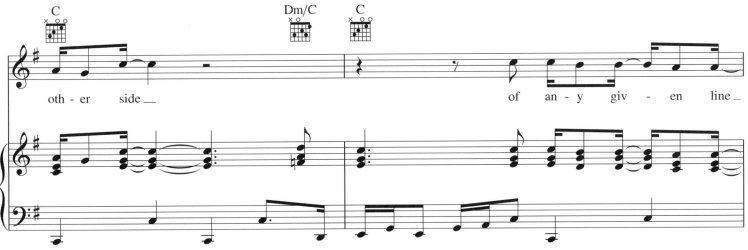

oth - er side _   of an - y giv - en line _

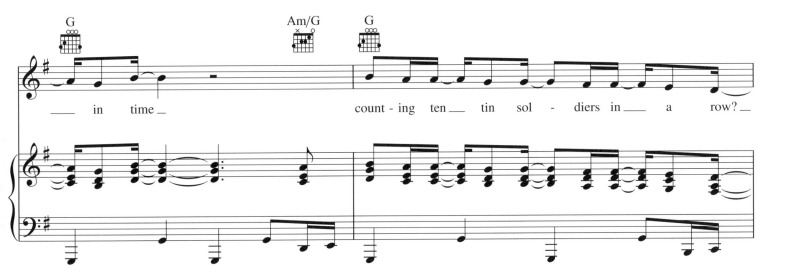

_ in time _   count - ing ten _ tin sol - diers in _ a row? _

_   Oh no, Ni - ki - ta, _ you'll nev - er _ know.

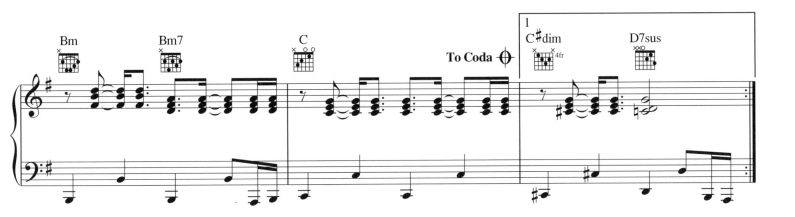

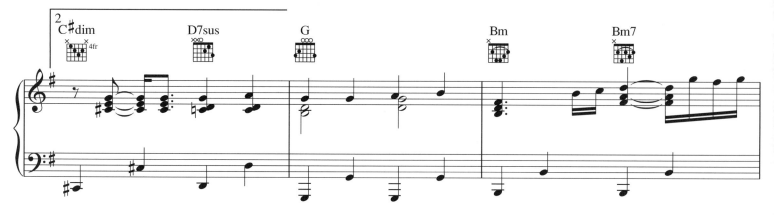

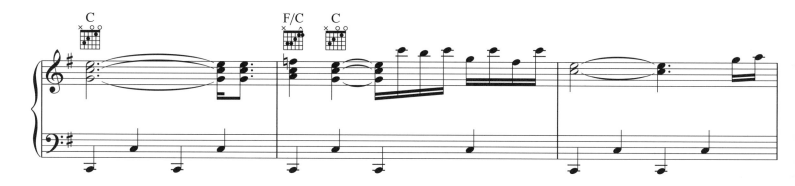

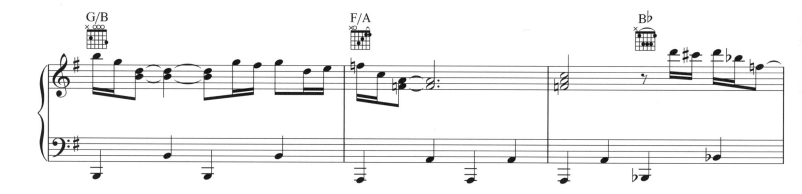

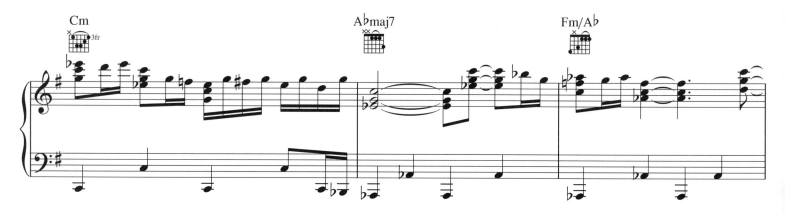

D.S. al Coda

Oh, Ni - ki - ta, you will nev -

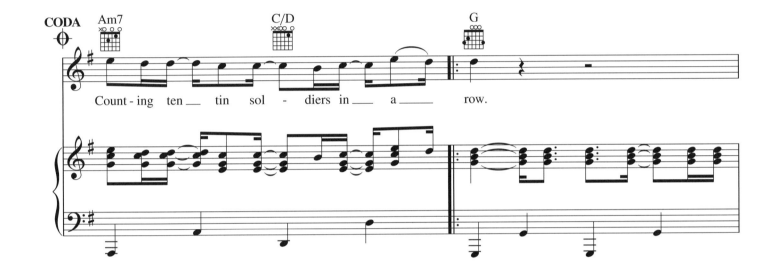

CODA

Count - ing ten __ tin sol - diers in __ a __ row.

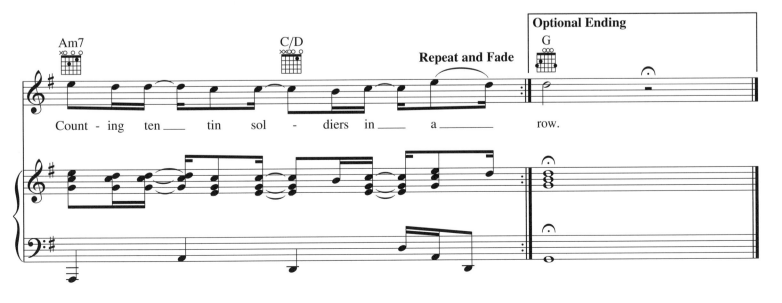

Repeat and Fade

Optional Ending

Count - ing ten __ tin sol - diers in __ a __ row.

THE ONE

Words and Music by ELTON JOHN
and BERNIE TAUPIN

Moderately slow Pop Ballad

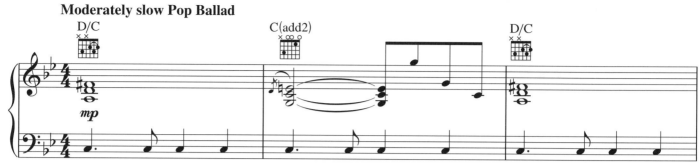

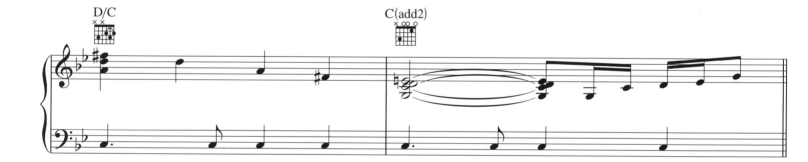

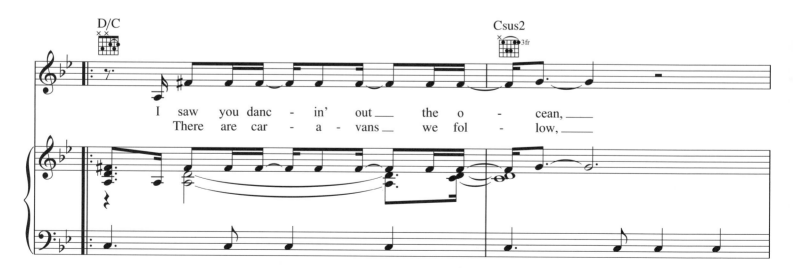

I saw you danc - in' out ___ the o - cean, ___
There are car - a - vans ___ we fol - low, ___

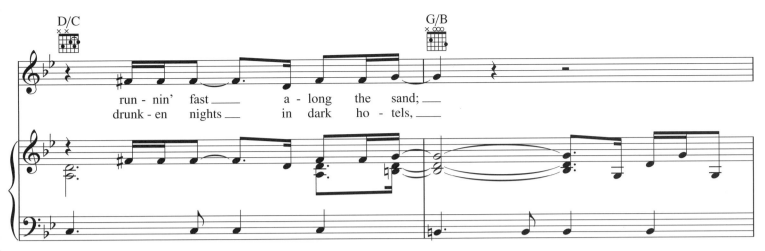

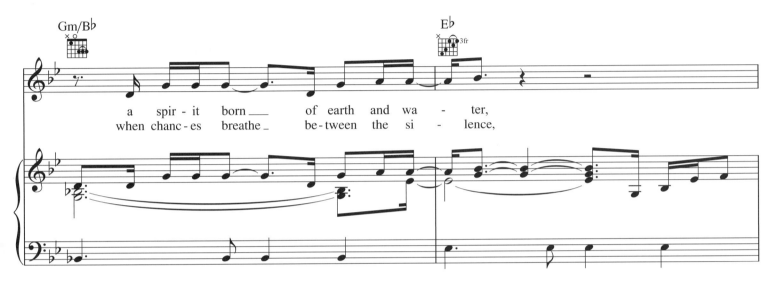

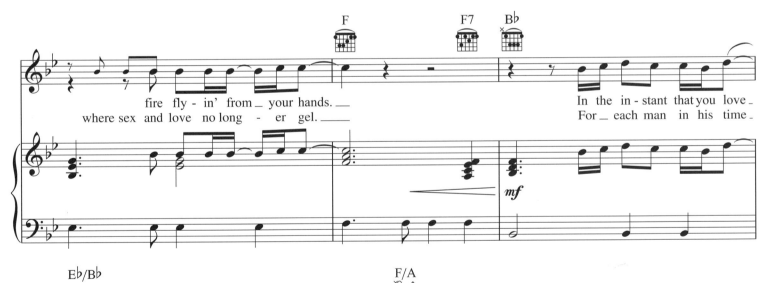

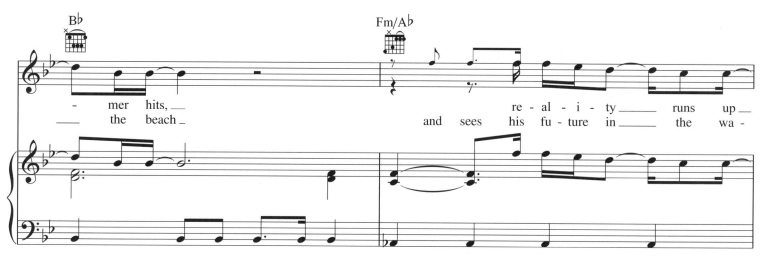

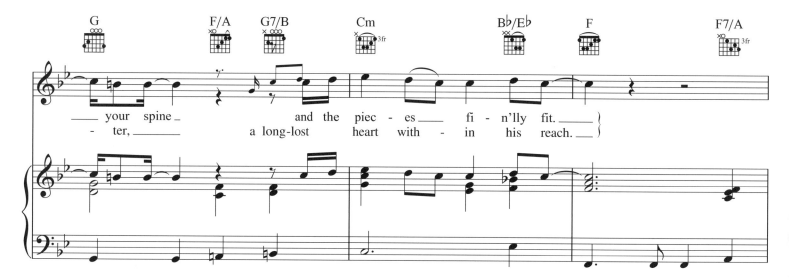

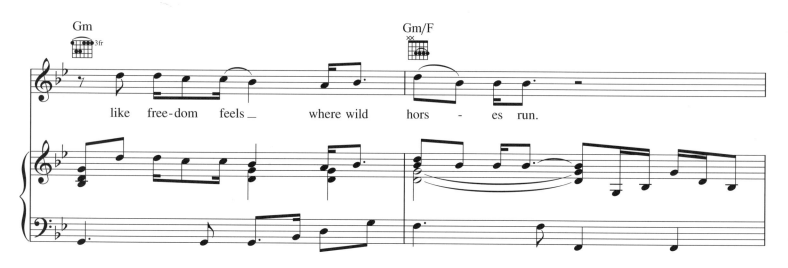

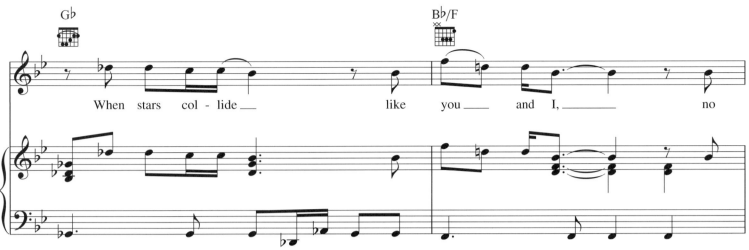

When stars col - lide ___ like you ___ and I, ___ no

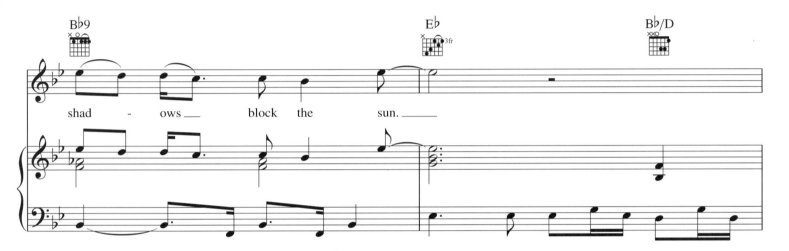

shad - ows ___ block the sun. ___

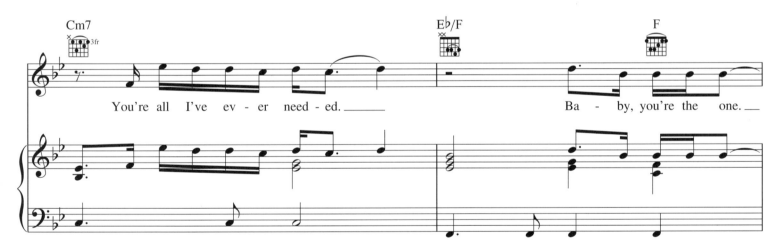

You're all I've ev - er need - ed. ___ Ba - by, you're the one. ___

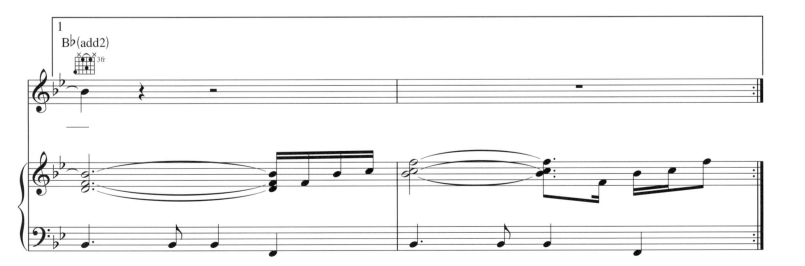

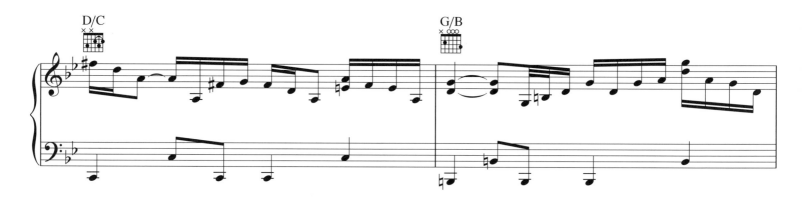

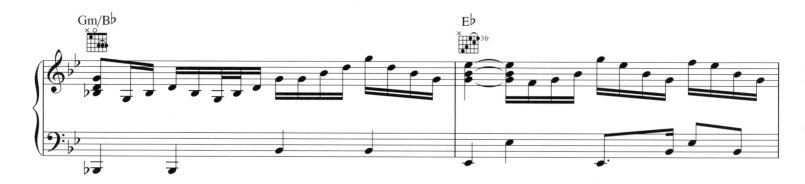

And all I ev-er need-ed _____ was the one,

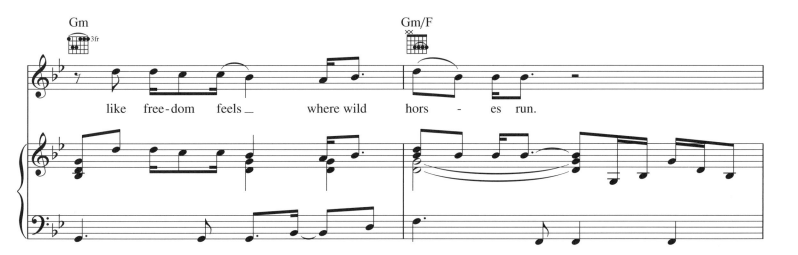

like free-dom feels _ where wild hors - es run.

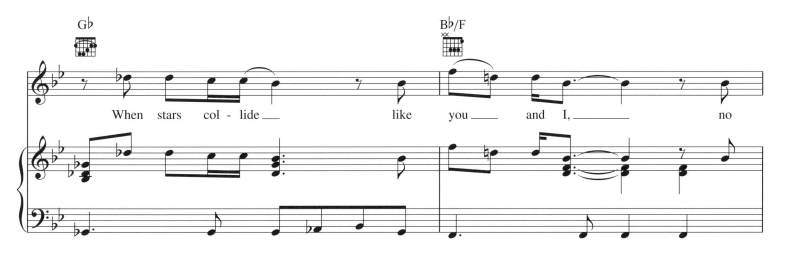

When stars col - lide _____ like you _____ and I, _____ no

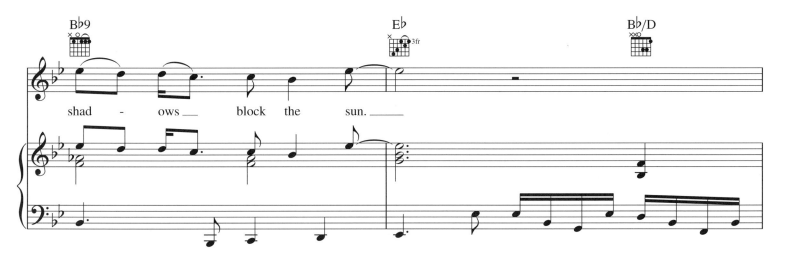

shad - ows _ block the sun. _____

You're all I've ev - er need - ed. _____ Ooh, ba - by, you're _ the one.

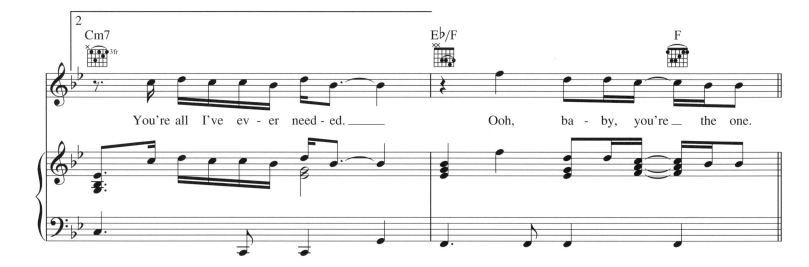

You're all I've ev - er need - ed. _____ Ooh, ba - by, you're _ the one.

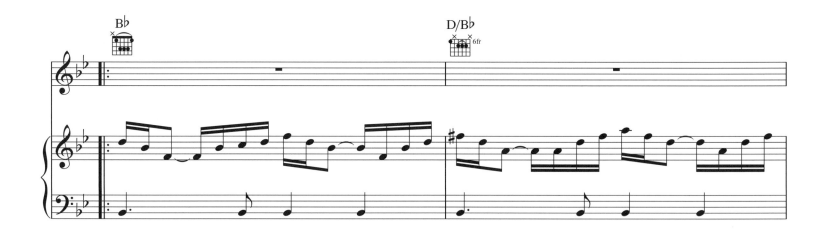

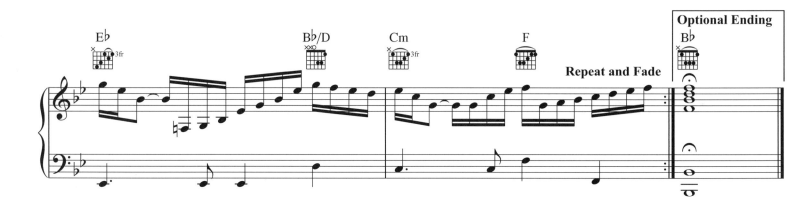

Optional Ending

Repeat and Fade

PLEASE

Words and Music by ELTON JOHN
and BERNIE TAUPIN

Moderately fast

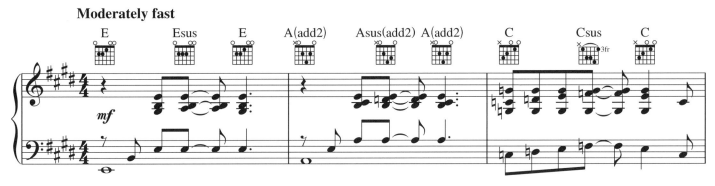

We've been crip-pled in love, _____
We've been liv-ing with sor-row, _____

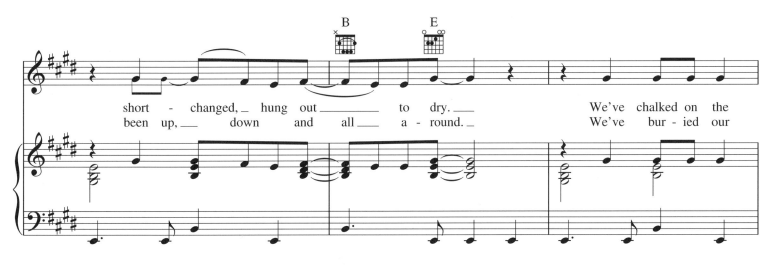

short - changed, ___ hung out _____ to dry. ___ We've chalked on the
been up, ___ down and all ___ a - round. ___ We've bur - ied our

walls _____ a slo - gan or two a - bout life. _____
feel - ings ___ a lit - tle too deep in the ground. _____ Stood dazed ___

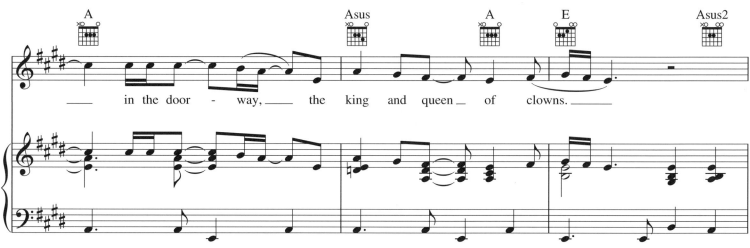

in the door - way, ___ the king and queen ___ of clowns. ___

We've been flipped ___ like a coin, ___ both ___ of us land - ing face-

down. _____ So _____ please, ___ please, ___ mm,

please, ___ let me grow old _____ with you. ___ Af - ter ev -

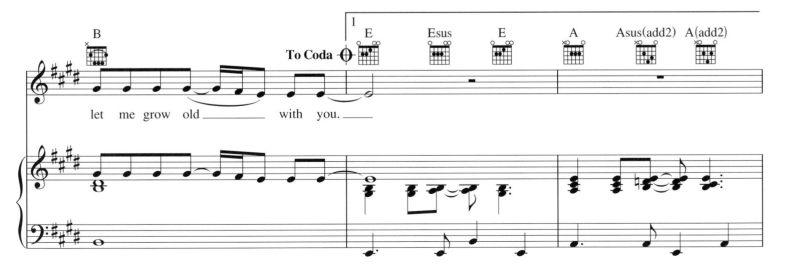

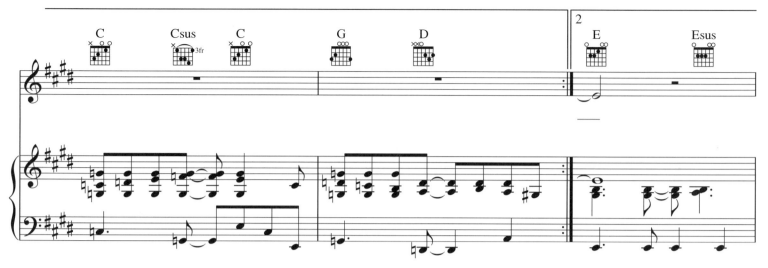

But tied to the same __ track, the two of us look __ back at

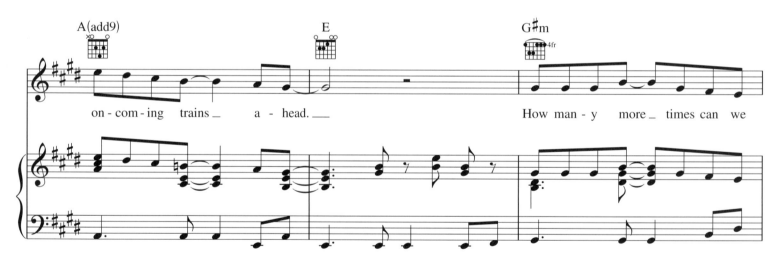

on - com - ing trains __ a - head. __ How man - y more __ times can we

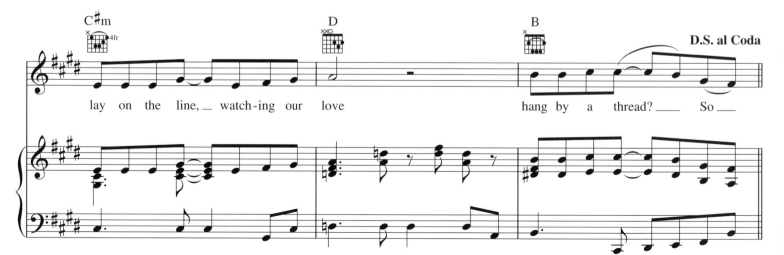

lay on the line, __ watch-ing our love hang by a thread? __ So __

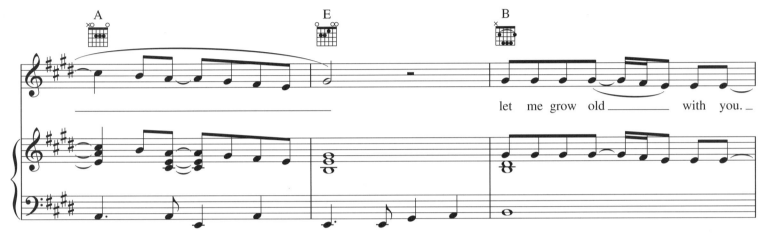

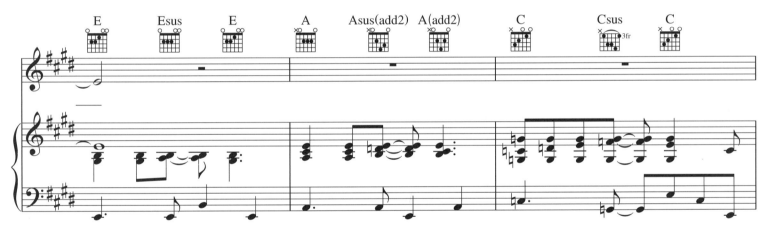

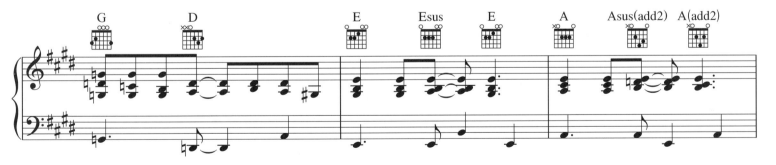

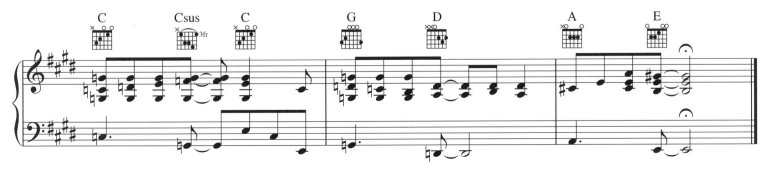

SOMEDAY OUT OF THE BLUE

(Theme from El Dorado)

from THE ROAD TO EL DORADO

Music by ELTON JOHN and PATRICK LEONARD
Lyrics by TIM RICE

Moderately, in 2

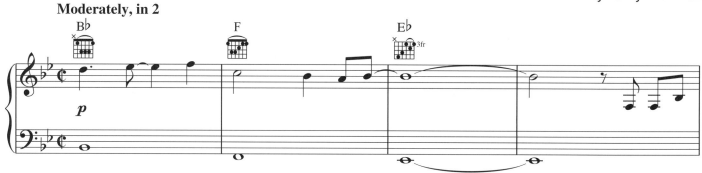

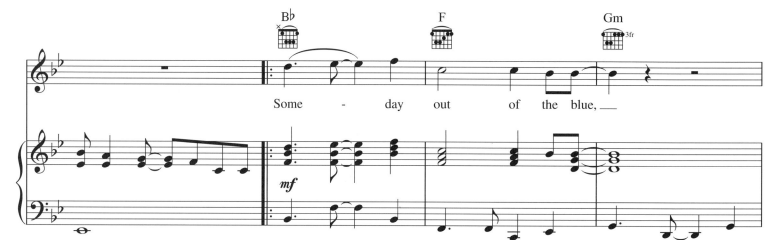

Some - day out of the blue, ___

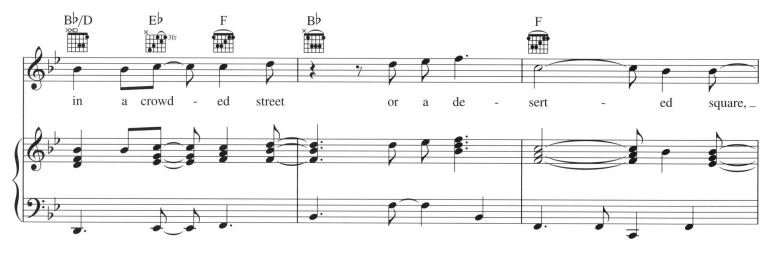

in a crowd - ed street or a de - sert - ed square, ___

___ I'll turn and I'll ___ see ___ you, as if our love ___ were ___

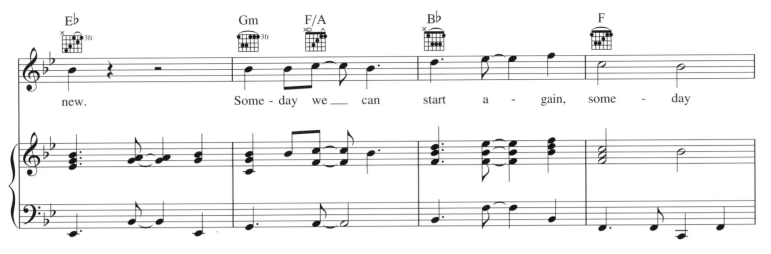

new. Some - day we __ can start a - gain, some - day

soon.

{ 1., 3. Here comes __ the night. __
{ 2. I still __ be - lieve, __

Here come the mem - o - ries. __ Lost in your arms, __
I still put faith __ in us. __ We had it all __

down in the for - eign fields, __ not so long a - go. __
and watched it slip __ a - way. __ Where are we now? __

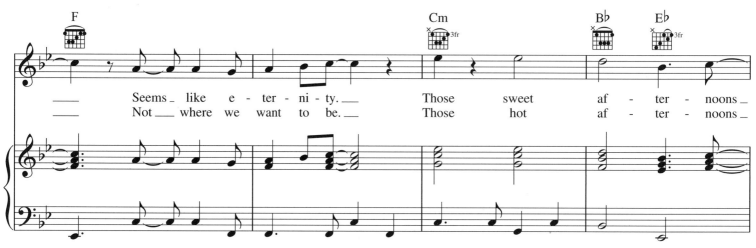

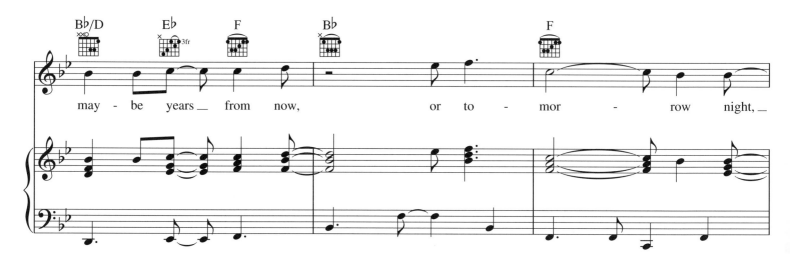

I'll turn and I'll __ see __ you, as if we al - ways __

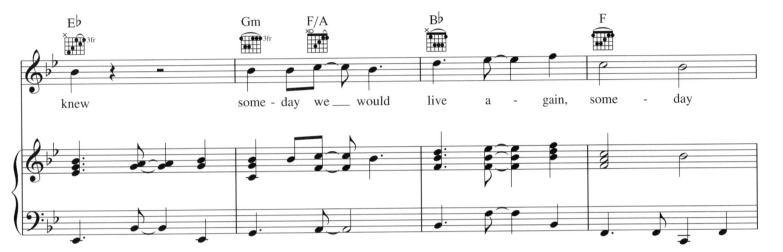

knew some - day we __ would live a - gain, some - day

soon. I still __ be - lieve, __

__ I still __ put faith __ in us. I still __ be - lieve, __

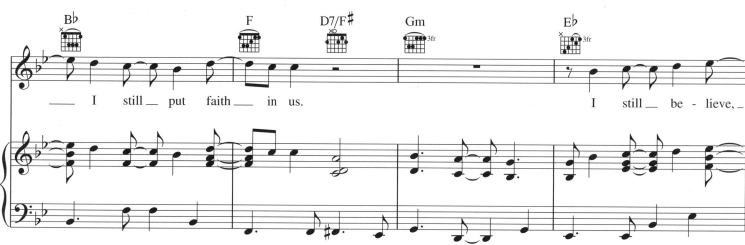

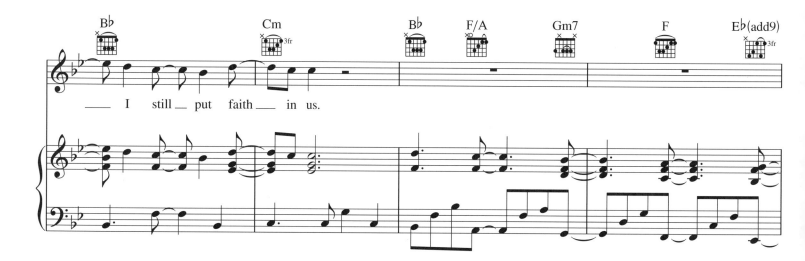

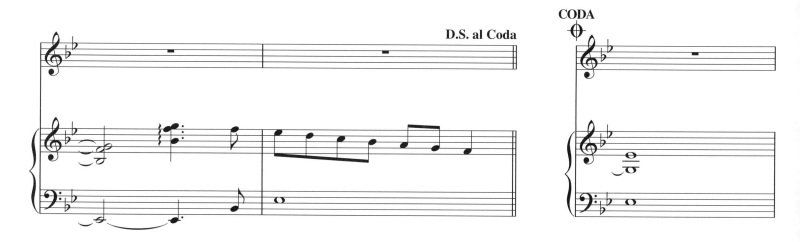

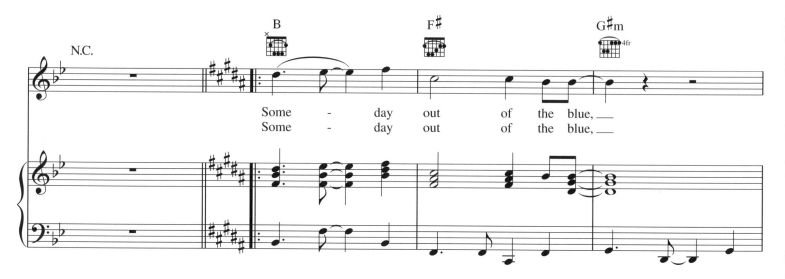

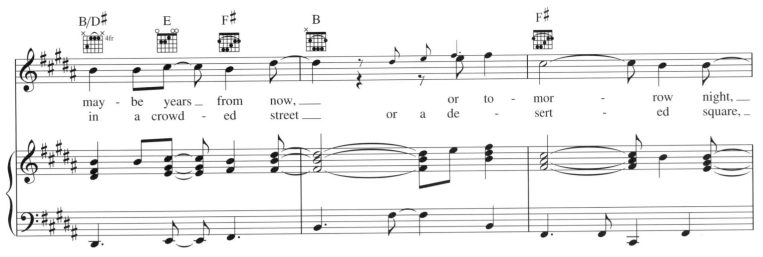

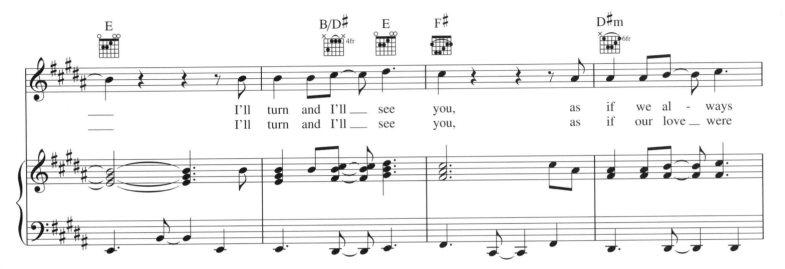

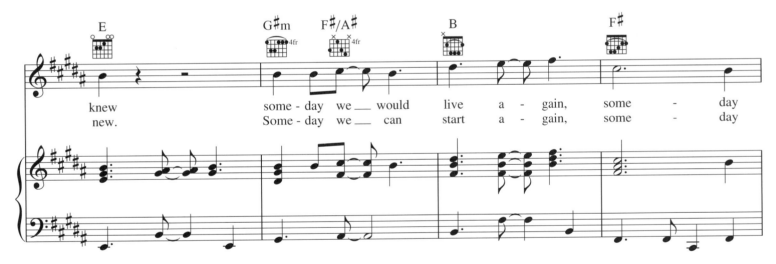

I still __ be - lieve, __ I still __ put faith __ in us.

I still __ be - lieve, __ I still __ put faith __ in us.

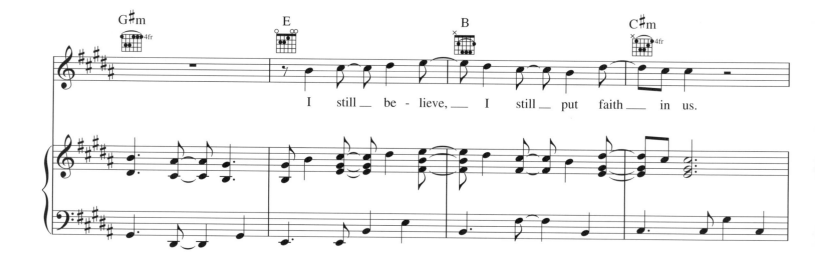

I still __ be - lieve, __ I still __ put faith __ in us.

Repeat and Fade

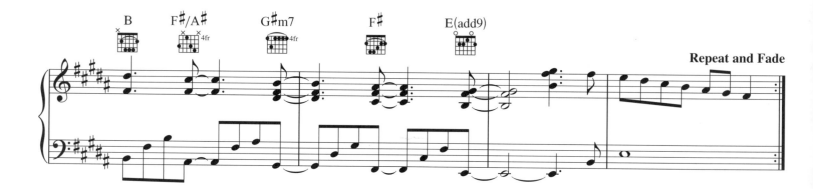

YOU CAN MAKE HISTORY
(Young Again)

Words and Music by ELTON JOHN
and BERNIE TAUPIN

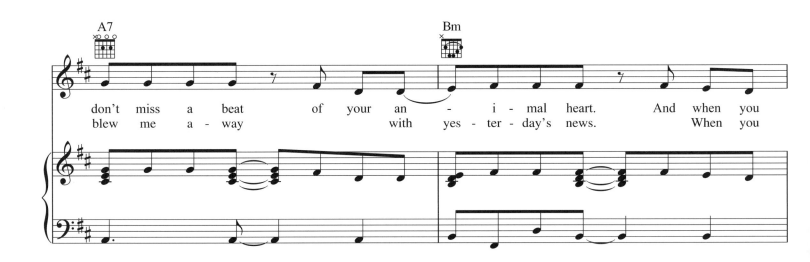

palm of my hand.) / hands of time.) Oh, babe, ___ you can make his - to - ry young ___

___ a - gain. ___ You could re - write __ it;

you could de - cide the things that should or should - n't have __ been. __

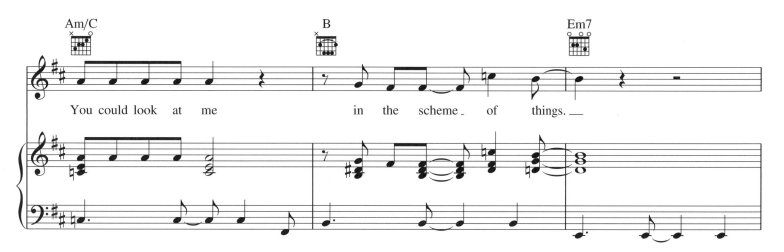

You could look at me in the scheme _ of things. __

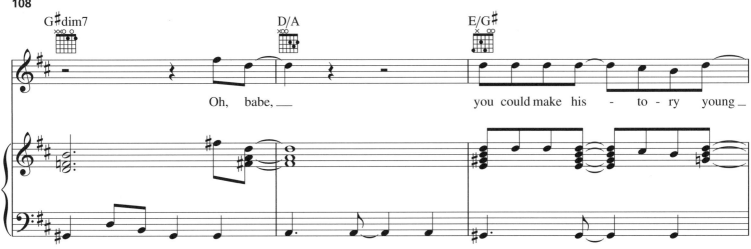

Oh, babe, ___ you could make his - to - ry young ___

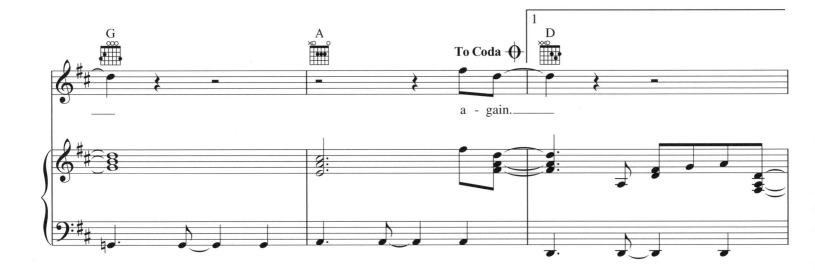

___ a - gain. ___

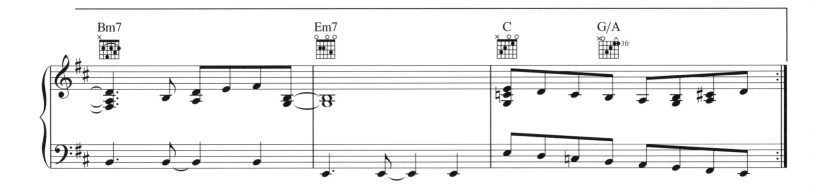

An - cient minds, ___ an - cient lives ___ got a

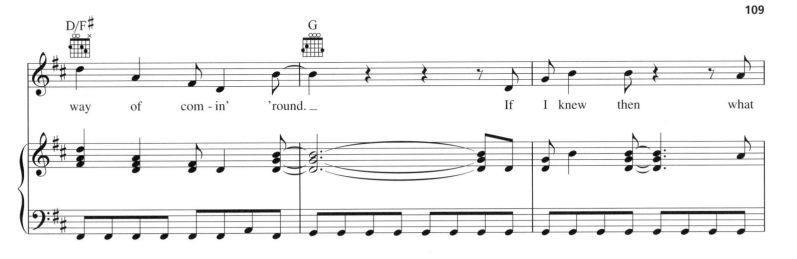

way of com-in' 'round. ___ If I knew then what

D.S. al Coda

I know now, ___ I'd make it back to you some-how. _____ Oh, babe, __

CODA

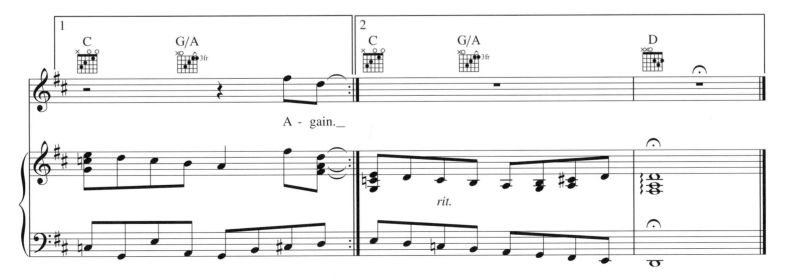

A - gain. __

rit.

SOMETHING ABOUT
THE WAY YOU LOOK TONIGHT

Words and Music by ELTON JOHN
and BERNIE TAUPIN

There was a time _____ I was
tell you _____ how you
smile, _____ you

ev - 'ry - thing __ and noth - ing all in __ one. __
light up ev - 'ry sec - ond all of the __ day, __
pull the deep - est se - crets from my __ heart. __

When you found me, _____
but in the moon - light, _____
In all hon - es - ty, _____

Recorded a half step higher.

I was feel - ing like ___ a cloud ___ a - cross the sun. ___
you just shine like ___ a bea - con of the bay. ___
I'm speech - less and ___ I don't know where to start. ___

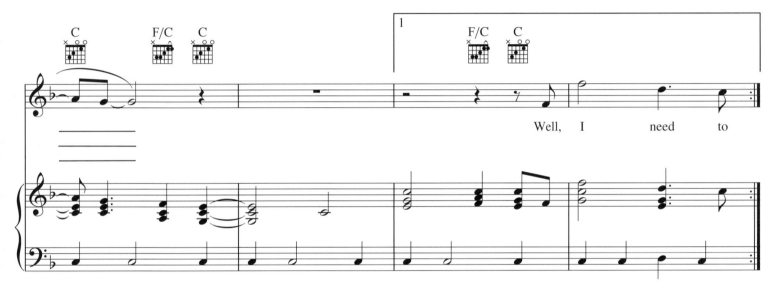

Well, I need to

And I can't ex - plain, _____

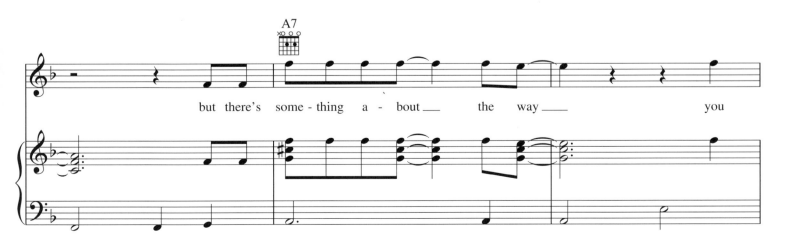

but there's some - thing a - bout ___ the way ___ you

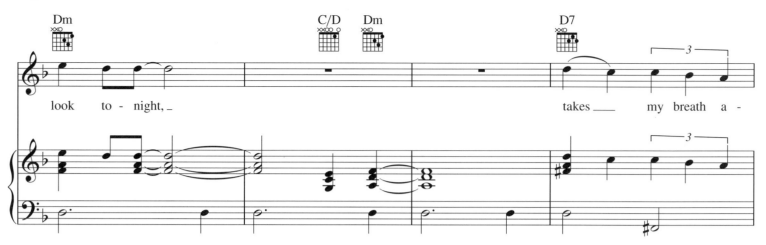

look to-night, _____ takes _____ my breath a-

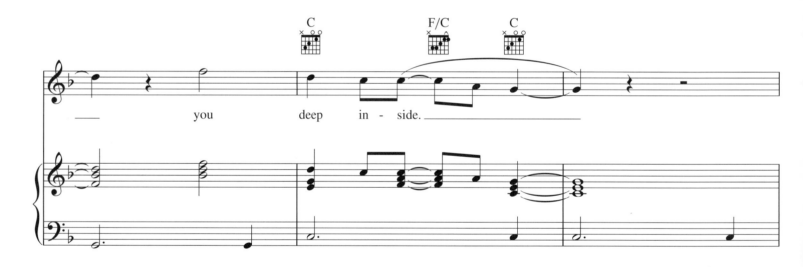

way. _____ It's that feel-ing I get _____ a-bout _____

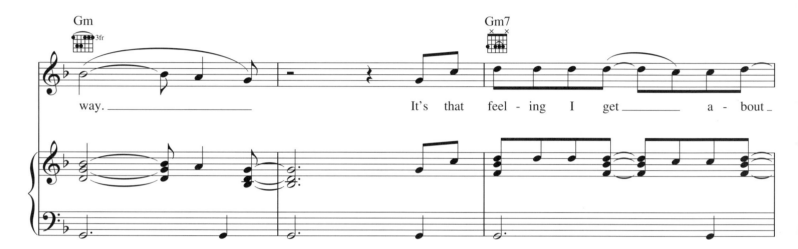

_____ you deep in-side. _____

And I can't de-scribe, _____

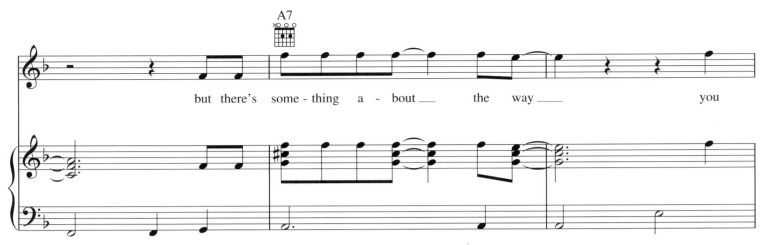

but there's some-thing a-bout ___ the way ___ you

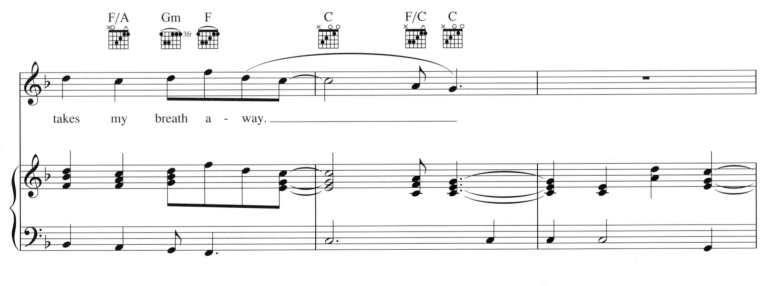

look to - night, ___

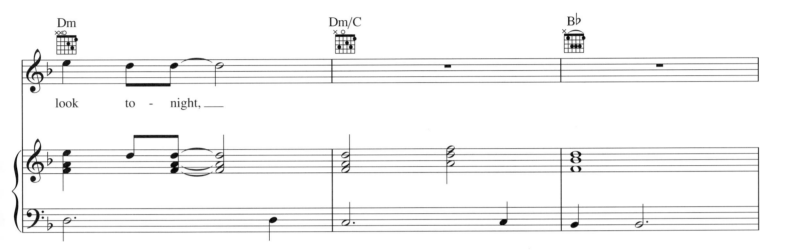

takes my breath a - way. ___

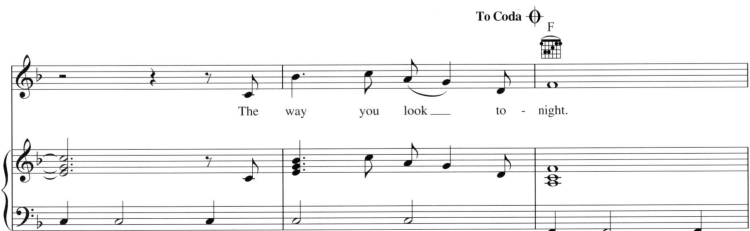

The way you look ___ to - night.

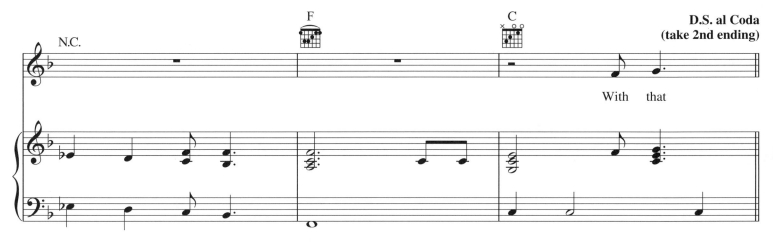

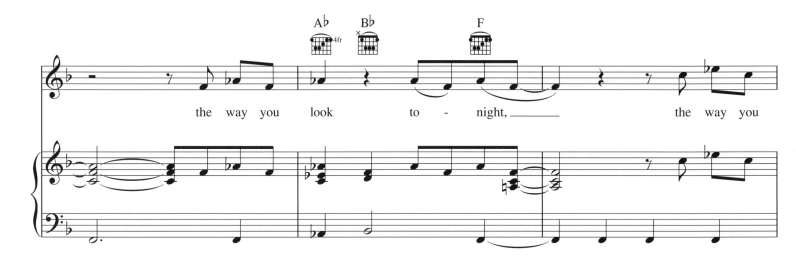

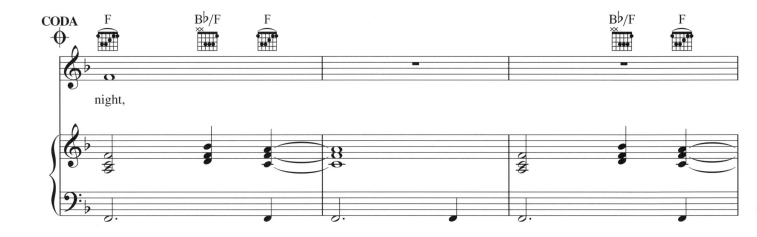

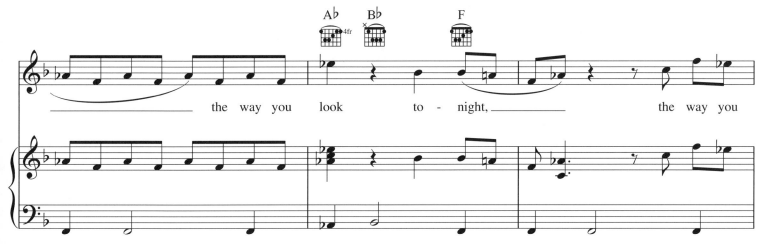

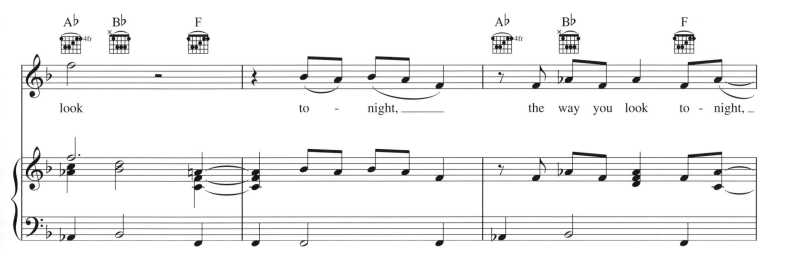

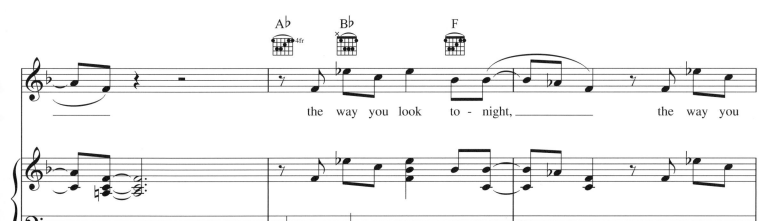

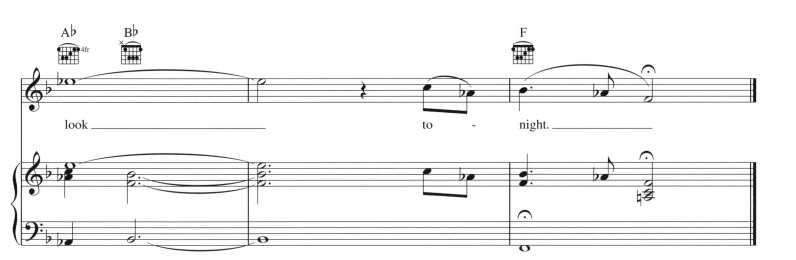

SORRY SEEMS TO BE THE HARDEST WORD

Words and Music by ELTON JOHN
and BERNIE TAUPIN

Gently, in 2

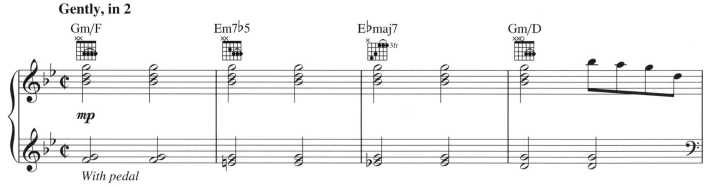

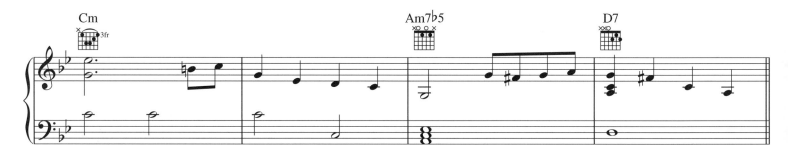

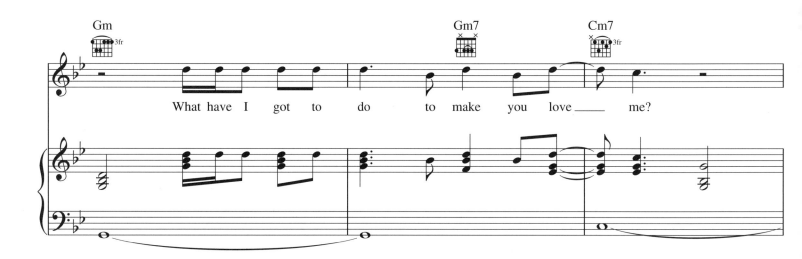

What have I got to do to make you love ____ me?

What have I got to do ____ to make you care?

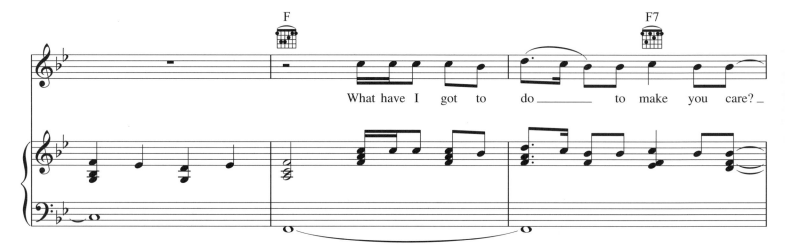

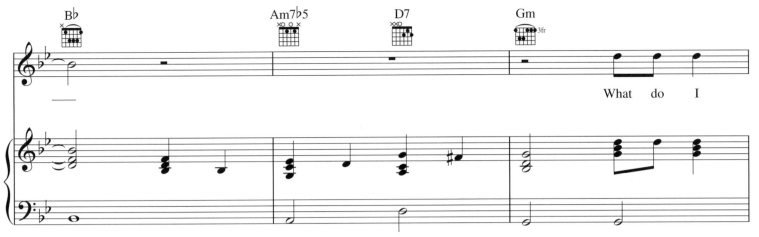

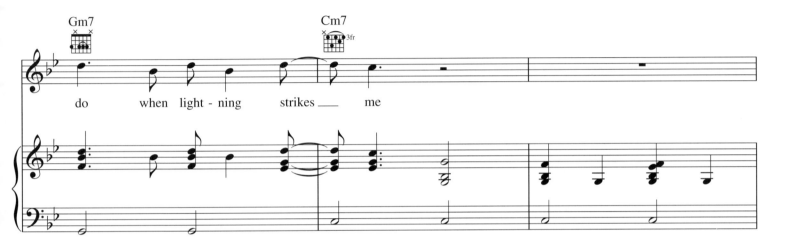

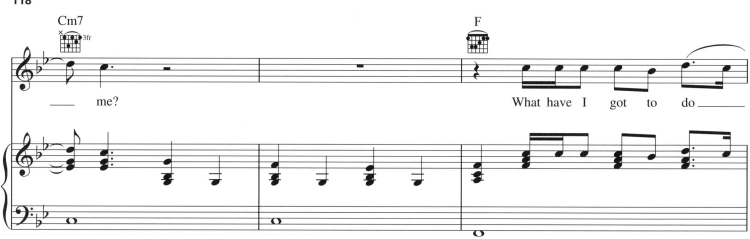

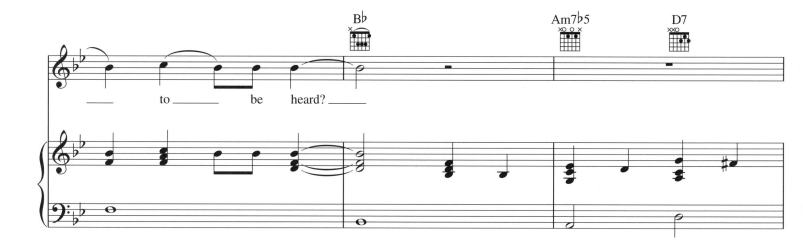

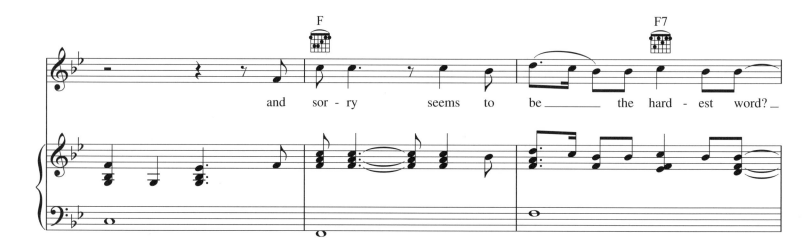

Why can't_ we talk ____ it o - ver? _____ Oh, it seems to me_

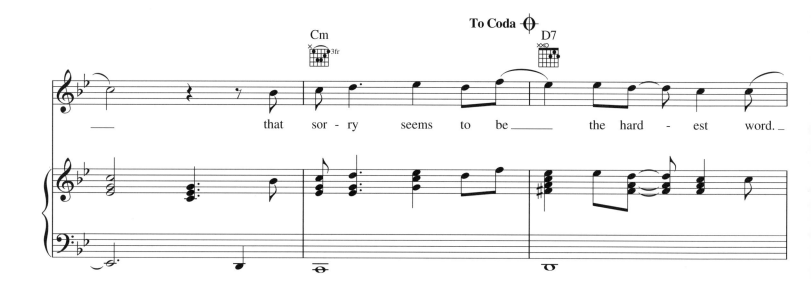

___ that sor - ry seems to be _____ the hard - est word. _

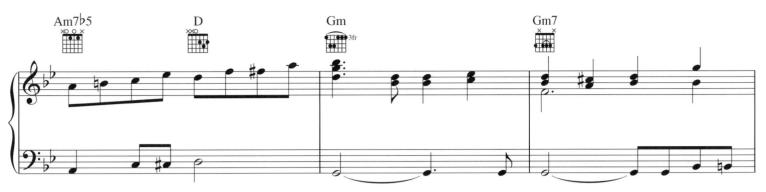

D.S. al Coda

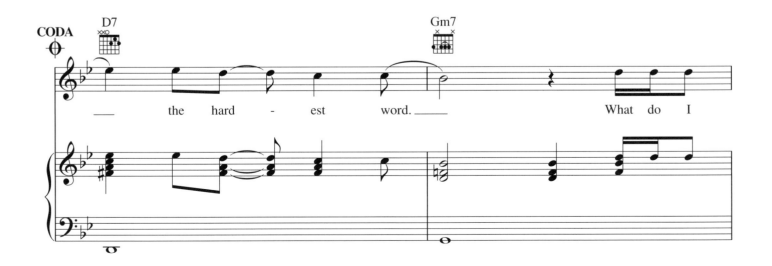

____ the hard - est word. ____   What do I

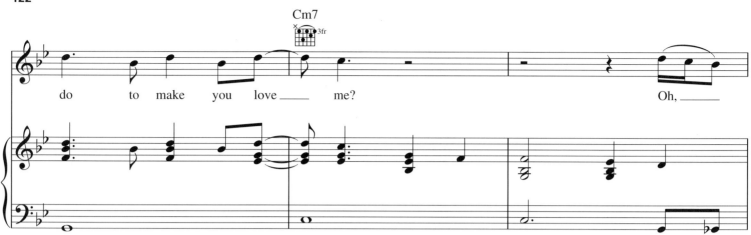

do to make you love ____ me?   Oh, ____

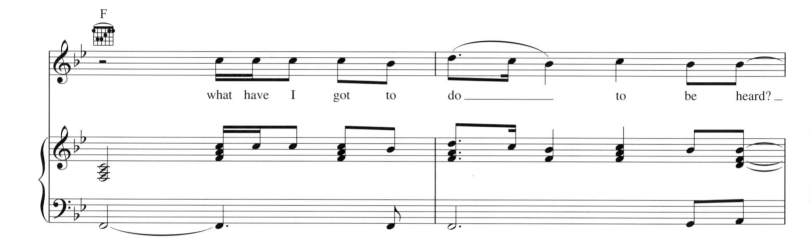

what have I got to   do _____ to be heard? __

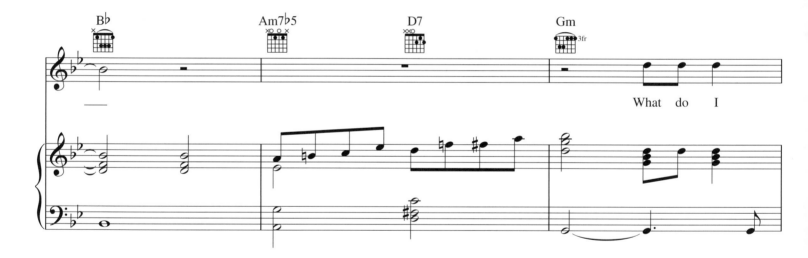

____   What do I

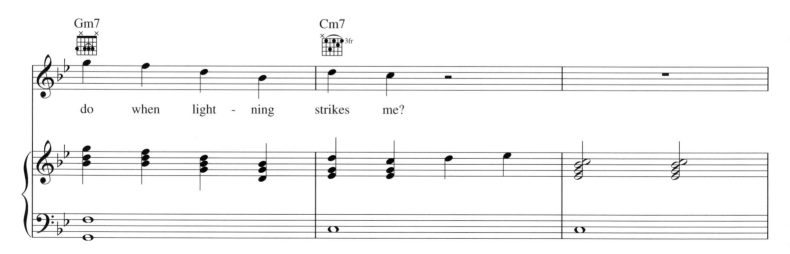

do when light - ning strikes me?

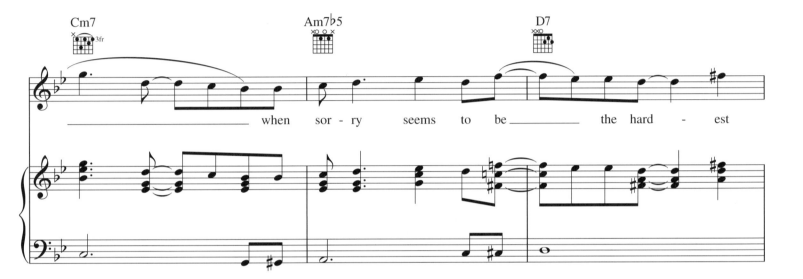

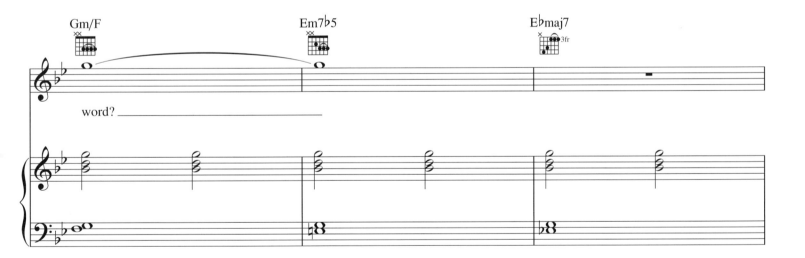

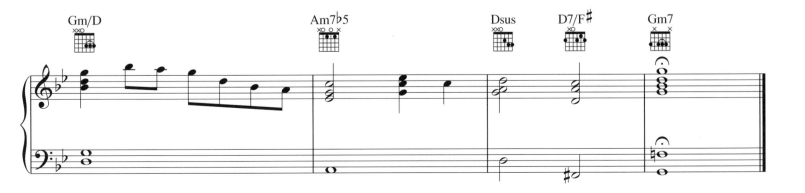

WHENEVER YOU'RE READY
(We'll Go)

Words and Music by ELTON JOHN
and BERNIE TAUPIN

Moderately fast

Oh, I

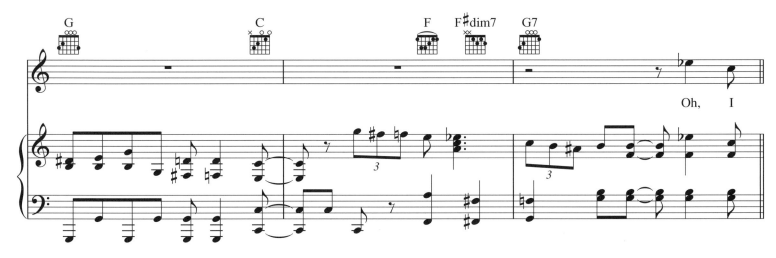

lived in a ten-e-ment six floors a-bove. I lent you my rec-ords and I

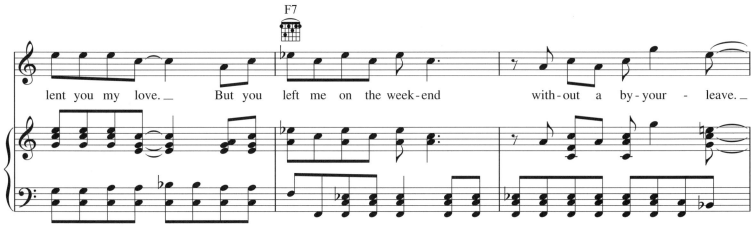

lent you my love. ___ But you left me on the week-end with-out a by-your-leave.

That's a dirt - y and a low-down trick; _

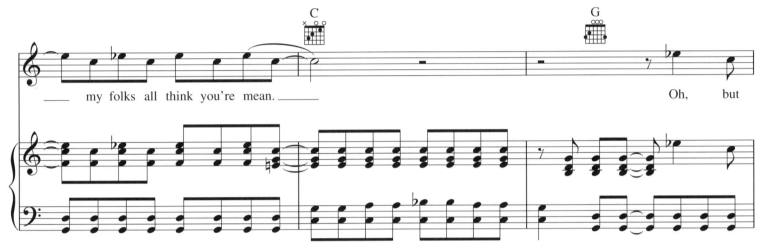

_ my folks all think you're mean. _____

Oh, but

I don't mind; ___ that's ___ kind of nif - ty. You

nas - ty with - out ____ you in my lit - tle old room. ___ I

al - ways see ___ those break - ups in the mov - ies. And just ___

miss you like cra - zy; please _ come back soon. I was

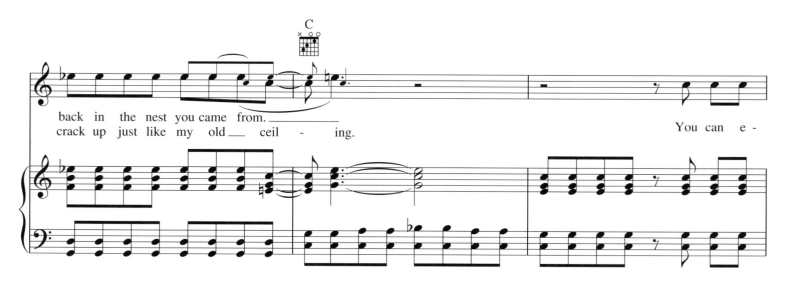

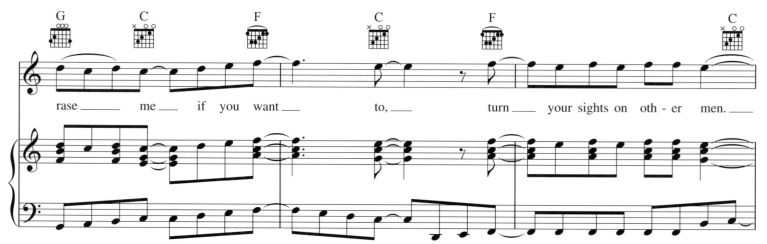

But when-ev - er you're read - y,

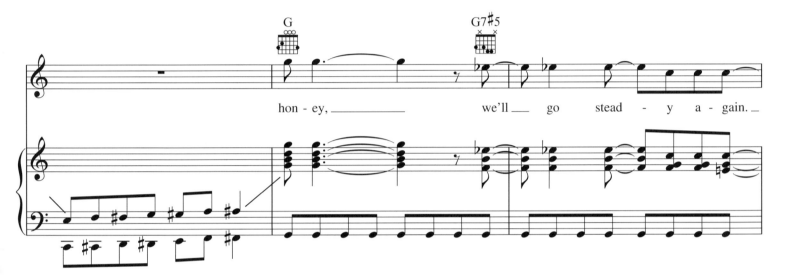

hon - ey, we'll go stead - y a - gain.

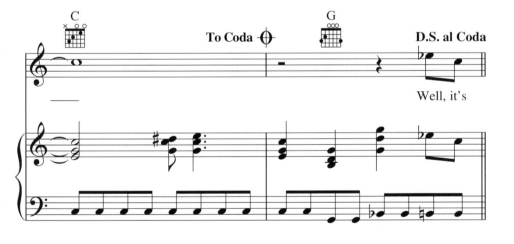

Well, it's

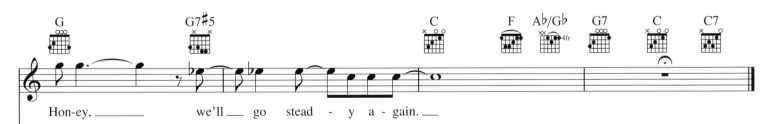

Hon-ey, we'll go stead - y a - gain.

WRITTEN IN THE STARS
from Elton John and Tim Rice's AIDA

Music by ELTON JOHN
Lyrics by TIM RICE

Male: I am here to tell ___ you we can nev-er meet a-gain. ___ Sim-ple real-ly, is-n't it? A word or two and then a life-time of not know-ing where or how or why or when. ___ You think of me or speak of me or won-der what be-fell ___ the some-one you once loved ___ so long a-

To Coda ⊕

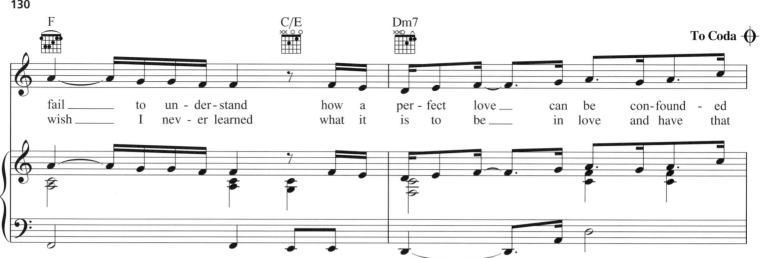

fail_____ to un-der-stand how a per-fect love ___ can be con-found-ed
wish _____ I nev-er learned what it is to be ___ in love and have that

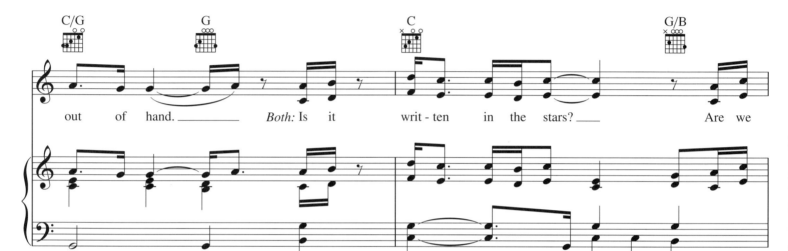

out of hand. _____ *Both:* Is it writ-ten in the stars? ___ Are we

pay-ing for some crime? _ Is that all that we are good for, ___ just a

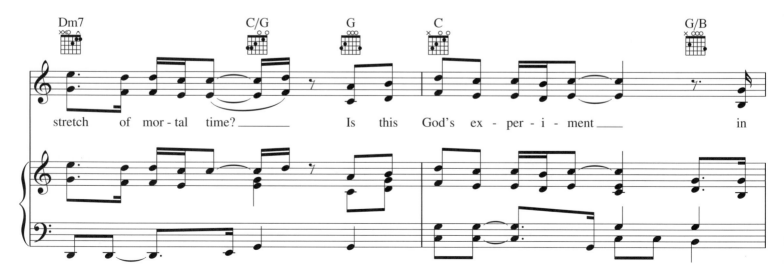

stretch of mor-tal time? _____ Is this God's ex-per-i-ment ___ in

which we have __ no say? __ In which we're giv-en par-a-dise, but

on - ly for a day. __

love re-turned. __ *Both:* Is it writ-ten in the stars? __ Are we

Oh __

pay - ing for some crime? __ Is that all that we are good for, __ just a

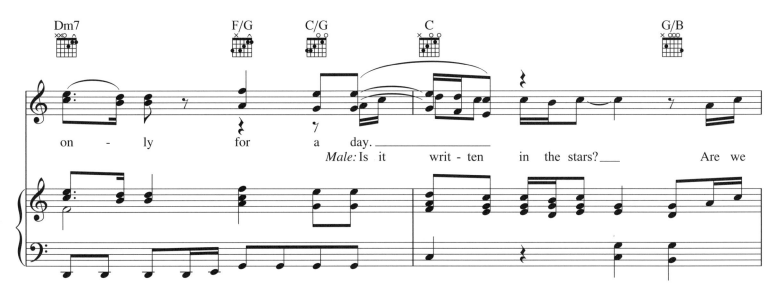

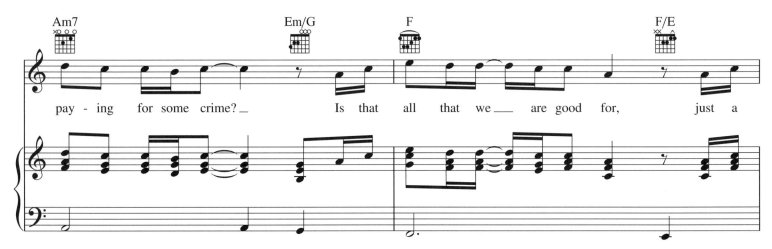

stretch of mor-tal time?___ *Both:* Is ___ this God's ex-per-i-ment _____ *Male:* in

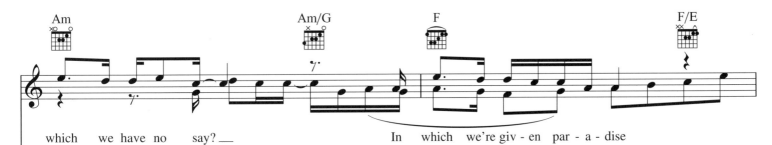

which we have no say?___ In which we're giv-en par-a-dise
Female: In which we have _ no say, _____ giv-en par-a-

on - ly *Both:* for a day. _____
dise _____

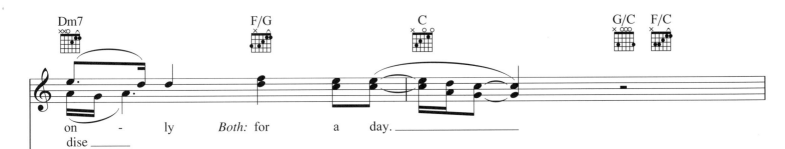

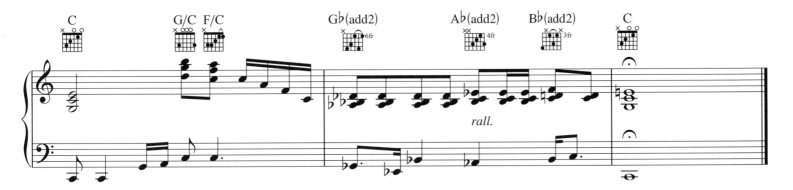

rall.

YOUR SONG

Words and Music by ELTON JOHN
and BERNIE TAUPIN

Moderate Ballad, in 2

It's a lit-tle bit fun-ny, ___
I sat on the roof ___

this feel-ing in-side. ___
and kicked off the moss. ___ Well, a few ___

I'm not one of those ___
of the vers-

who can eas-i-ly hide. ___ I
-es, well, they've got me quite cross. ___

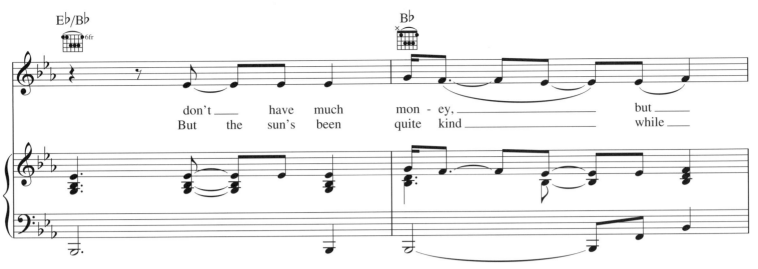

don't ___ have much mon - ey, _____ but _____
But the sun's been quite kind _____ while ___

boy, if ___ I did, _____ I'd buy ___ a big
I wrote _ this song. _____ It's for peo - ple like

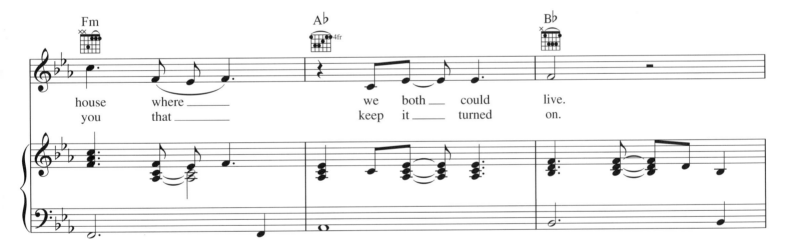

house where _____ we both ___ could live.
you that _____ keep it ___ turned on.

If I was a sculp - tor,
So ex - cuse me for - get - ting,

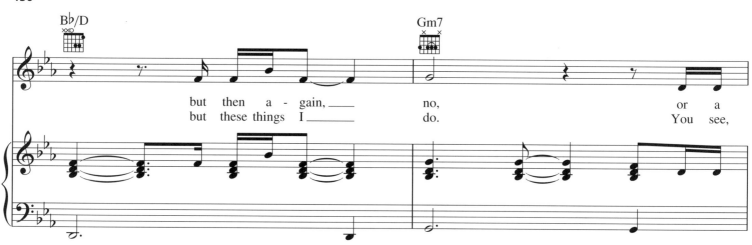

but then a - gain, _____ no, or a
but these things I _____ do. You see,

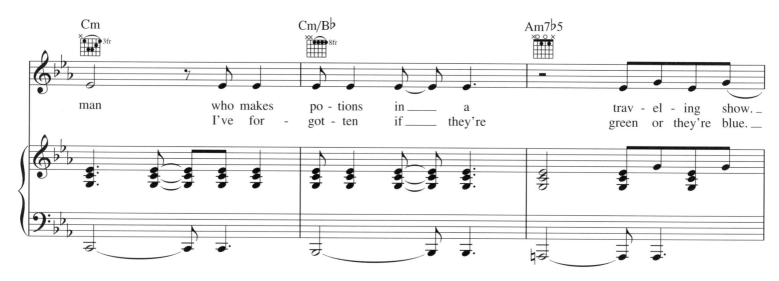

man who makes po - tions in _____ a trav - el - ing show. _____
I've for - got - ten if _____ they're green or they're blue. _____

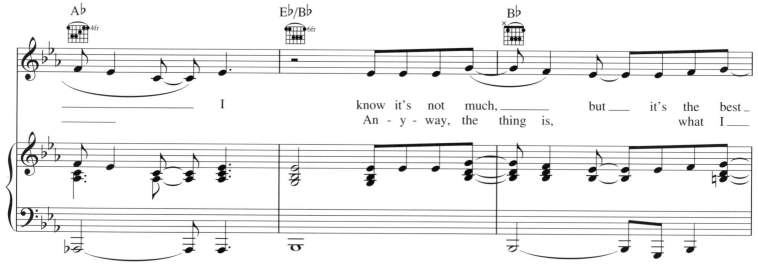

_____ I
_____ know it's not much, _____ but _____ it's the best _____
An - y - way, the thing is, what I _____

_____ I _____ can do. _____
_____ real - ly mean, _____ My gift _____ is my
yours are the

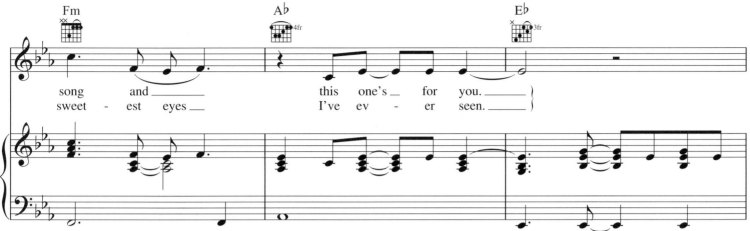

song and _____ this one's __ for you. _____
sweet - est eyes ___ I've ev - er seen. _____

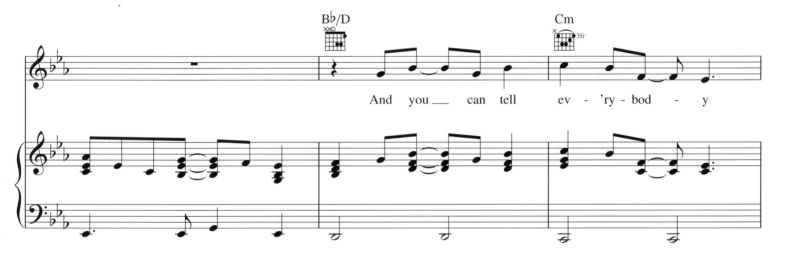

And you __ can tell ev - 'ry - bod - y

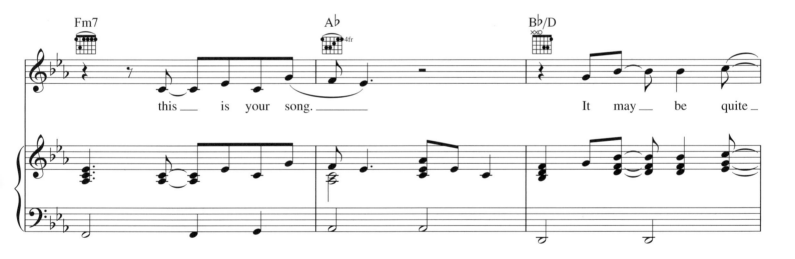

this __ is your song. _____ It may __ be quite __

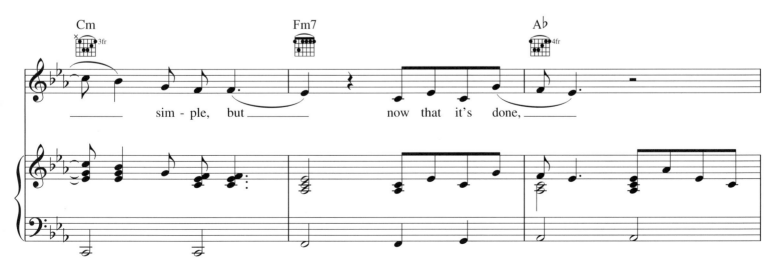

_____ sim - ple, but _____ now that it's done, _____

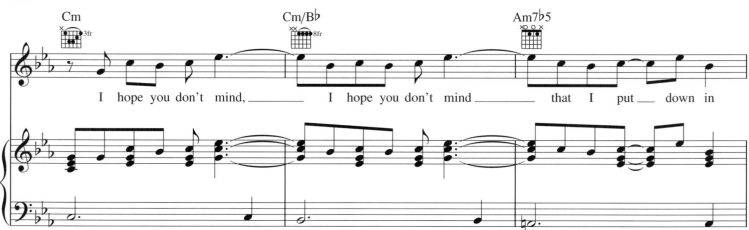

I hope you don't mind, _____ I hope you don't mind _____ that I put _____ down in

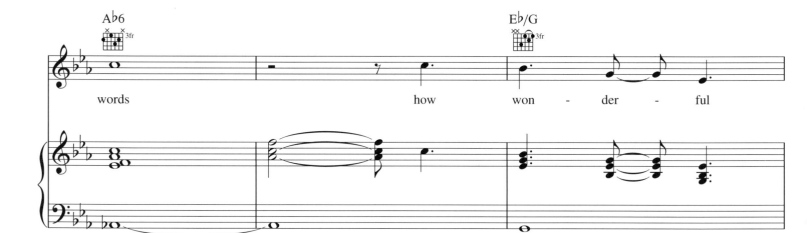

words _____ how won - der - ful

life is _____ while you're _ in _____ the world. _____

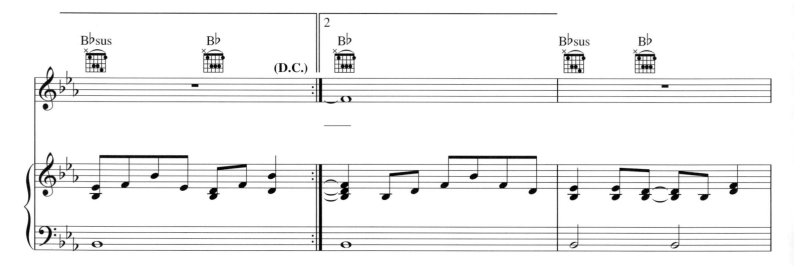

(D.C.)

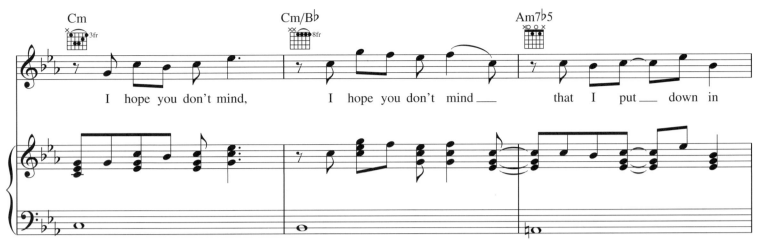

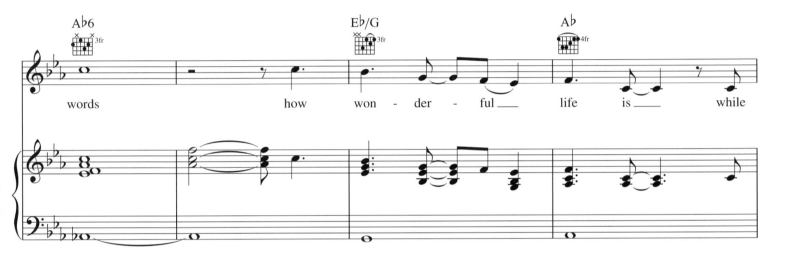

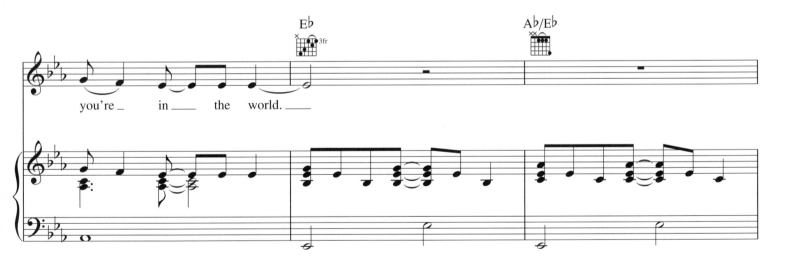

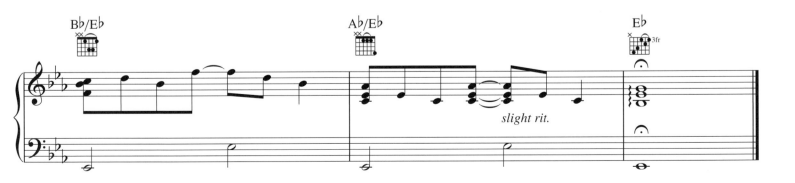

YOU GOTTA LOVE SOMEONE

featured in the Paramount Motion Picture DAYS OF THUNDER

Words and Music by ELTON JOHN
and BERNIE TAUPIN

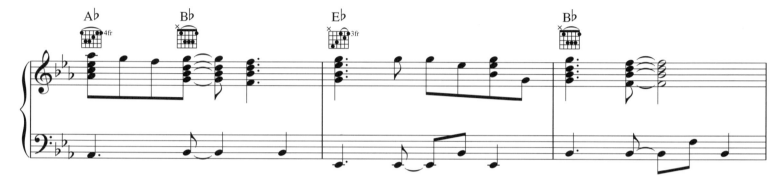

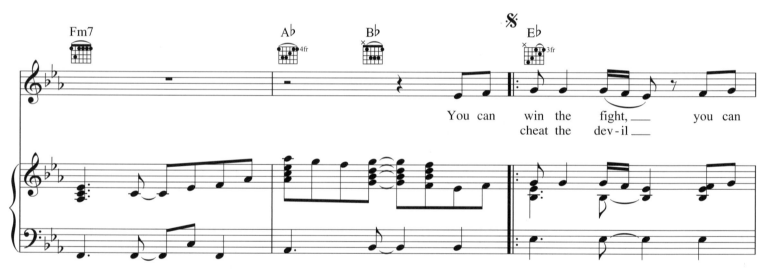

You can win the fight, ___ you can
cheat the dev-il ___

grab a piece of the sky. ___
and slice a piece of the sun. ___

You can

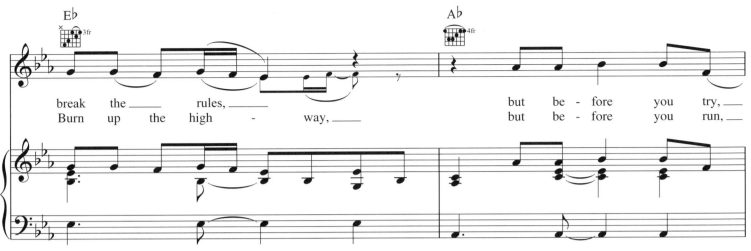

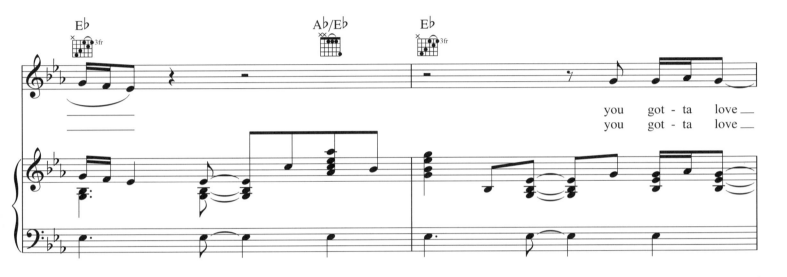

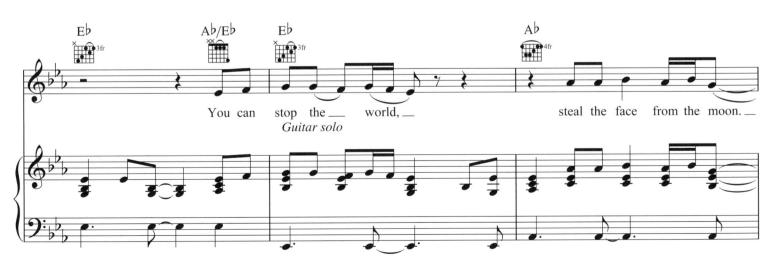

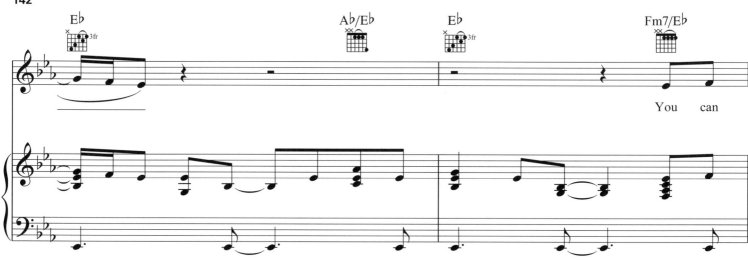

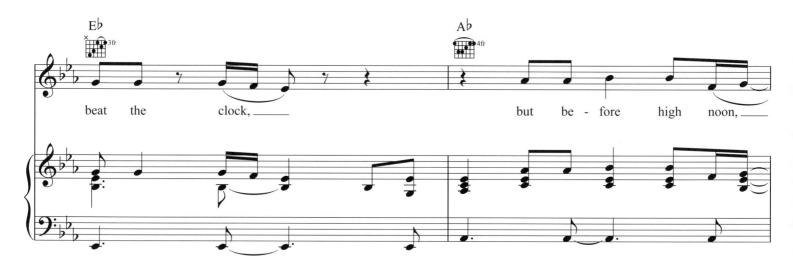

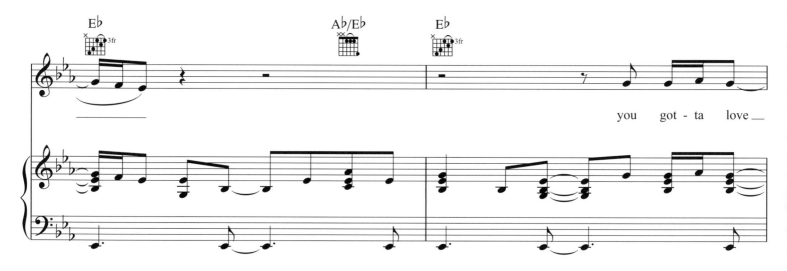

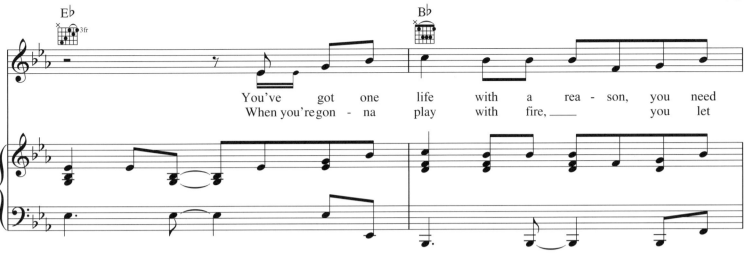

You've got one life with a rea - son, you need
When you're gon - na play with fire, _____ you let

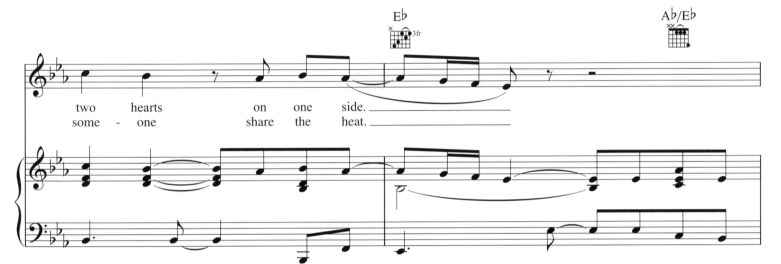

two hearts on one side. _____
some - one share the heat. _____

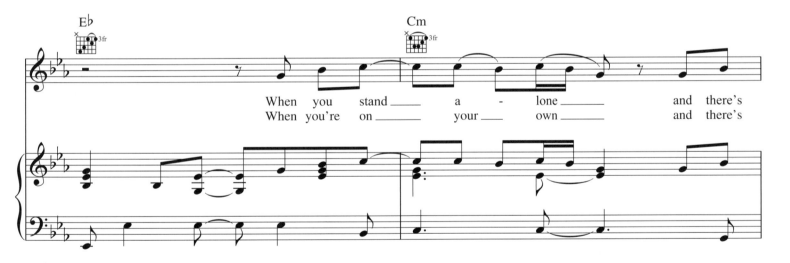

When you stand _____ a - lone _____ and there's
When you're on _____ your _____ own _____ and there's

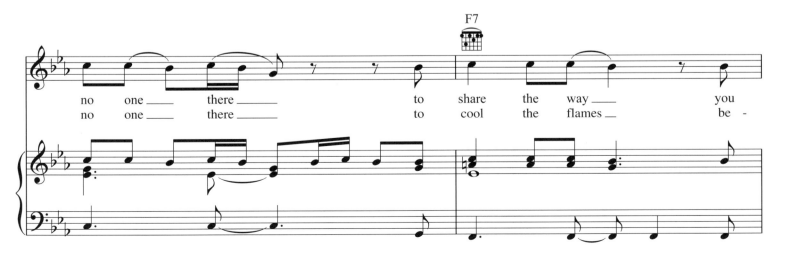

no one _____ there _____ to share the way _____ you
no one _____ there _____ to cool the flames _____ be -

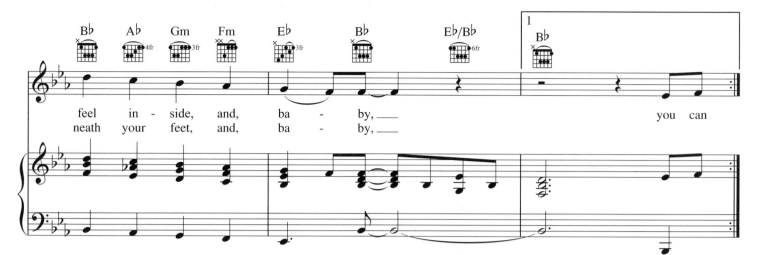

feel in - side, and, ba - by, ___ you can
neath your feet, and, ba - by, ___

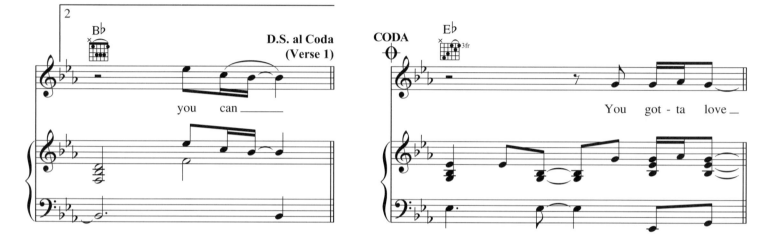

you can ___

You got - ta love ___

___ some - one. ___

You got - ta love ___ some - one. ___

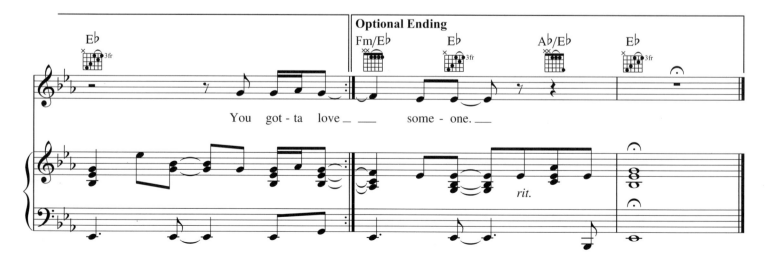

You got - ta love ___ some - one. ___